The Stevie Wonder Scrapbook

The Stevie Wonder Scrapbook

by Jim Haskins
with Kathleen Benson

Grosset & Dunlap
A Filmways Company
Publishers New York

ACKNOWLEDGEMENTS

Grateful acknowledgement is made to the following people for their help in making this book possible: Daa'iyah Ali, Mary Ellen Arrington, Kwame Braithwaite, Jim Cummins, Julie Davis, Alix DeJean, Ellen Inkelis, Rochelle Larkin, Basil Phillips, Ira Tucker, Kathy Benson. . .and Stevie Wonder.

Photograph on page 1 by Wide World Photos.
Photograph on title page © 1978 by Kwame Brathwaite.

Designed by Marcia Ben-Eli

Published simultaneously in Canada
Library of Congress catalog card number: 78-53021
ISBN 0-448-14464-6 (hardcover)
ISBN 0-448-14465-4 (paperback)
Printed in the United States of America
First printing 1978

Contents

See, about sound . . . there's one thing you gotta remember about sound—sound happens all the time, all the time. If you put your hands right up to your ears, if you close your eyes and move your hands back and forth, you can hear the sound getting closer and farther away . . . sound bounces off everything.

—Stevie Wonder

(Kwame Brathwaite)

1

The Early Years

Fifteen miles down the Saginaw River from Saginaw Bay in eastern Michigan lies the city of Saginaw, population 91,000. It is only ninety miles away from giant Detroit, home of the automobile, so naturally it is a manufacturing center, producing auto parts, metal products, fabricated metals and machinery to serve the auto industry. Its people are primarily blue-collar factory workers, and like the people of Detroit, if the automobile were outlawed or were suddenly to become otherwise extinct, they would find their survival seriously jeopardized. They depend on modern technology just as their forbears depended on nature. They do not worry much about ecological concerns. They want to be happy, to have a house and a television and a car and some of the other good things in life. As such, they are essentially indistinguishable from other urban midwesterners, and Saginaw, Michigan, would be indistinguishable from countless other factory towns across the United States were it not for the occurrence of a simple, unheralded event some three decades ago. On May 13, 1950, Steveland Morris was born there.

Sometimes he liked to be alone, to go to the park on a nice day and play his harmonica to the accompaniment of the rustling leaves. He would grow up loving to visit quiet parks to get away from the hectic pace of his life. (Paul Slade, *Pictorial Parade*)

His birth was four weeks premature. A few generations earlier, he would not have lived, but in 1950 there was technology available to keep him alive for the vital month until he could grow big enough to survive. An incubator kept the tiny infant in a constant temperature of 80° F., or higher, with constant humidity and an ample supply of oxygen. The trouble was that little Steveland Morris got too much oxygen during that first month of his life in the man-made womb; and although his life was saved, his eyesight was destroyed forever. In 1950 doctors did not realize the damage to the eyes that too much oxygen could cause, particularly to the eyes of a premature, underweight infant. As a direct result of the overdose of oxygen, Stevie was left with retrolental fibroplasia, an opaque fibrous membrane behind the lens of each eye. Working its faulty magic, as it has done so often, in its even-handed way technology saved the child's life and blinded him at the same time. But Stevie was lucky; a premature baby girl born in the hospital at the same time died.

(Ebony)

No one knows what Stevie Wonder's life might have been like if he hadn't been blind. For blind though he is, he has still fulfilled some of the highest expectations of the American dream, which dangles the promise that since all men are born equal, all can aspire to exchange their rags for riches. It is a dream infrequently realized, but Stevie Wonder has come from what he describes as "upper lower circumstances" in Saginaw and in Detroit, where the family moved when he was a small child, and on from Motown to international stardom. A spirituality, a love for the world and its people, a belief in goodness are what power him. And those beliefs together with high energy and great talent as a performer, built upon a solid foundation of technical skill, have carried Stevie Wonder to the top.

When you look at the photograph of Stevie with his mother at the 1974 Grammy ceremonies where he collected four awards, you see the strong, proud face of a woman who years earlier knew that her child was blind, and was determined to see that he would do more with his life than make potholders or brooms, or clank his way through the world with a guide dog and a metal cup for quarters and dimes.

Survival was a struggle for the family during the early years of Stevie's life. He remembers everyone going out to a dry dock to steal coal so they could keep warm in the bitter Saginaw winters.

Stevie's father had once told his older brother Calvin that Saginaw was only twelve miles from the North Pole. And the winter climate being what it was, Calvin and his brothers had gone around telling everyone this important fact of life, until someone put them right. "We were poor all right," says Stevie, "but I wasn't aware of it as much as other kids would be. Being blind I didn't see the things I didn't have, like on television, for example. I was sort of lucky."

So successful was Stevie's mother, now Mrs. Lulu Hardaway, in raising her son as a normal child that he was four years old or so before he began to realize one of his senses was missing. When he bumped into walls or furniture, he thought only that he wasn't as good at getting around as his two older brothers or his parents. And his brothers, not really understanding his blindness either, worked their way around his handicap in the straightforward manner that children have. If he couldn't play catch, if an incident had to be described for him, there were a dozen different kinds of mischief he could get into, and he did so with enthusiasm.

On one occasion his brothers decided that what Stevie needed was more light. He remembers their having a garbage can and some matches in the house and saying, " 'Maybe we can set this thing . . . like start a fire in here and he'll have more light.' So they went and started a fire and almost burned the house up." They got "whumped," all three of them, something which happened quite often to lively Stevie.

He recalls that he first realized he might be different from others when he stepped in dog leavings in the back yard, and his mother bawled him out, and told him he must not roam about so much. Even then, it was the curtailing of his liberty that he noticed, more than any definite awareness of what the word *blind* meant. Stevie managed to do the things that most small boys do if they can. He climbed trees to steal apples, and he jumped from the roof of one woodshed to another, guided by his developing "sonar." He found that if he shouted, he could gauge how far away the other rooftop was by the way his voice bounced back. He even learned to ride a bicycle, and took along a sighted passenger to act as guide. "I always have loved my mother for giving me that independence," he says; "[she] let me feel the breeze of riding a bicycle."

As a baby and a very small child, Stevie's mother took him along to faith-healers, hoping desperately for a cure. He was prayed over, his eyes were touched by people who believed themselves to

be in direct contact with God, who believed that the child's affliction could be cured through the power of prayer and faith. But even while she prayed and hoped for a miracle, Stevie's mother was raising him to be independent, to take care of himself, as a kind of insurance against the reality she knew he would have to deal with one day. Since she had to go to work each day to support her children he was forced to be more self reliant than many blind children would have been. Stevie was well cared for as a child, but he was never babied. As a result, people say of Stevie today, as they have said all his life, that he is sightless yes, but not blind. He even turns the light on and off as he enters and leaves the bathroom, because he hears other people doing it, and he has adopted this habit from the sighted world, one of the many things he does which make him seem less than blind in the accepted sense of the word. His engineer in Los Angeles, John Fischbach, says, "He can hit you with a roll of tape from across the room." He roller-skates, he swims, he bowls, and he plays air hockey (a game played with a paddle and a puck which is kept afloat by air currents). He can pick up a conversation across a crowded room, and that sonar system, developed from the time when he jumped from one rooftop to the next, prevents him from bumping into walls and other objects whose presence he can "hear."

It is typical of Stevie that very early in his life he took control of his own destiny. Knowing that his mother prayed for sight to be given to him, and knowing she was unhappy that he could not see, he told her one day that he was happy being blind, that he thought it was a gift from God. He still sees it this way, as a gift from God that has made it necessary for him to search for and find forms of expression that the sighted can live without, to reach further inside himself. He says, "Being blind, you don't judge books by their covers; you go through things that are relatively insignificant, and you pick out things that are more important." Blind people spend more time in their inner world than do the sighted. There is no night or day for them; their time is governed by the sounds that other people make—the click of the light switch that tells a blind child it is time to sleep, the clatter of dishes in the kitchen that tells him breakfast is on the way. He cannot see, but he can tell when someone passes him; the swish of air, the passing smell, the sound of footsteps. He remembers not a face, but a handshake and a voice. When Stevie was a kid adults would drop a nickel, a quarter

The warmth of the sunshine on a spring day, the soft furry coat of a puppy—these were some of the things that made each day an adventure for Stevie. (Paul Slade, *Pictorial Parade*)

or a dime on the table and say, "What's that, Stevie?" And he would pick up on the particular sound, the particular tune played by the coin, and identify it.

"I can feel the cycle of the sun going up and down," says Stevie, "I can feel the world spinning 'round."

All small children like nothing better than to bang a tin pot with a spoon. They enjoy the physical activity, the fun of being in charge of a loud sound, stopping it, starting it, banging out their own rhythms. But those who remember Stevie as a tiny child remember him as wanting to bang out those rhythms more. It seemed as though he must make music in some fashion each and every day of his life. "I was always beating things, like beating on tables with a spoon, or beating on those little cardboard drums they used to give kids. I'd beat 'em to death."

He quickly learned how to play a four-note toy harmonica that one of his uncles gave him. He would hear a tune, then go to work trying to get it out of the harmonica, making music as best he could, frustrated when the sounds in his head wouldn't come out of the little instrument.

When the family moved to Detroit, Stevie soon became known in the neighborhood. A nearby barber, noticing how he loved music, and how he tried so hard with his four-note harmonica, gave him a real one. A new world of possibilities opened up for Stevie, he had the instrument that would give him the music he heard on the radio. By the time he was eight years old Stevie was proficient on the bongos, the harmonica, the drums and the piano.

It seemed as though fate conspired to keep Stevie supplied with instruments so that he could learn and grow as a musician. Perhaps it was simply that genius shows up at an early age, and is unmistakable when it is present. (Mozart was writing music at four, after all.) Perhaps it was that compelling quality in Stevie which caught people's attention.

When he was in the first grade, the Lions Club gave a Christmas party for blind children, and having heard that Stevie wore out toy drums regularly, they gave him a set of real drums. He sat down then and there and went to work! He was able to learn to play the piano, something unheard of for a poor black child living in the Detroit ghetto, because a neighbor was moving out of the project and didn't want to take her piano with her. Because of his frequent impromptu concerts on neighborhood stoops, when he would imitate the musicians he admired, Stevie's neighbor must have known that he would put the piano to good use. He remembers asking his mother, " 'When they gonna bring the piano over, Mamma?' I never realized how important that was going to be to me." And when it finally arrived, there was the feeling of the smooth wood, the new set of smells and textures which said, Piano. In no time he was trying his hand at the B. B. King tunes he heard on the radio. With his set of drums, his harmonica, his piano and his radio, more and more Stevie created his own world, a world of music. But there were other worlds with which he had to cope, and in Detroit he encountered the outside, racially conscious world.

He was enrolled in an elementary school for the blind. Though integrated, it was predominantly white, and Stevie quickly learned that at school, although everyone there was blind or partially so, he was different in another way because he was black. Although it was never stated outright, when the subject of the future came up, when possibilities for life success for the students were discussed, Stevie recalls an undertone "that made me feel like because I was black I could never be or would never be [successful].

"I used to listen to this black radio station in Detroit on my way to school," he remembers. "Like I was the only black kid on the bus, and I would always turn the radio down, because I felt ashamed to let them hear me listening to B. B. King. But I *loved* B. B. King. Yet I felt ashamed because—because I was *different* enough to want to hear him and because I had never heard him anywhere else."

Although Stevie could not see difference in skin color, he had begun to learn that such difference existed, that there were white people and black people and that they lived for the most part in different worlds. He would hear his parents talk about white people who treated black people badly, who regarded them as inferior, who stopped them from getting jobs, who prevented them from living in nice neighborhoods with trees and space. He learned that the white children always seemed to have more of everything, mythical refrigerators stuffed with food, more toys at Christmas, more clothes, more shoes.

I remember sitting by the television, and hearing, 'Get this Hostess Twinkie' with kids smacking their lips and saying, 'Oooh, it's good!' And I remember kids in school saying, 'Look what I got

Because he could not see, Stevie had to learn through his other senses. To him, "policeman" meant the feel of a metal badge. (Paul Slade, *Pictorial Parade.*)

for Christmas!' It did make me wish I could have those things. But now, I just like the basic things of life—to have an instrument, something really fascinating to the ear or something educational. Or to be warm and comfortable with the person I love."

But he has never forgotten riding that school bus with his radio turned low to stay out of trouble. "Freedom," he says, "begins in the simplest things, even in such things as feeling free enough to turn on a radio to a particular station. You have to seize that for yourself and then demand that kind of freedom for others."

Stevie's school experience, of course, was more than learning about racial and economic differences. It was also learning how to cope with his blindness. Under the tutelage of his teachers, he learned to speak more clearly, to show on his face his feelings and moods, and to make better use of his sense of touch. He learned braille, and when he had mastered the system would be rewarded with a braille Bible. But his favorite subjects were math and typing. He was also encouraged to increase the acuteness of his hearing, although in that area he needed little encouragement. He had shown an early interest in the possibilities of the human voice and was already adept at mimicry. Within a year or two after the move to Detroit, his baby brother, Larry, had been born, and it was Stevie who was first able to identify the meaning of the baby's vocal sounds for the rest of the family. As early as the second grade, Stevie was showing considerable advancement in aural acuity. One day, his teacher heard a mouse but could not seem to locate it. She asked her students to be very quiet and try to listen for it. Though they could all hear it, none could seem to locate the source of the sound. Then Stevie spoke up. "It's in the wastepaper basket!" he announced, and sure enough, it was.

No doubt his intense interest in music was the major source of his highly developed sense of hearing.

The radio was his lifeline, introducing him to worlds of music he would never have known about otherwise. "I spent a lot of time listening to the radio," he says, "and I was able to relate to the different instruments and know what they were. I began to know them by name. I used to listen to this program on station WCHB . . . called 'Sundown.' The disc jockey was named Larry Dixon and he always played a lot of old songs. There was one thing he played, it was his theme song . . . 'da da duh duh *dommm* da duh . . . da da da da *dommm dommm* da da duh . . .' Oh, it's really a bad tune, really a beautiful song—can't think of the name right now, but I could never forget that tune." One of his earliest memories was of Johnny Ace singing "Pledging My Love." "I played Jimmy Reed's blues, Bobby Blue Bland's. I used to sit by the radio and listen till sunup. Took a little of everybody's style and made it my own."

Among his numerous other musical influences was church music. As a member of the choir of the Whitestone Baptist Church he received invaluable musical training. Learning what it meant to combine with others to make music was excellent discipline for a young musician. He soon went on to singing lead parts, and that led to his being named a junior deacon.

Stevie loved to play music on any kind of instrument. He became proficient on drums and bongos at an early age, and enjoyed giving porch concerts in his Detroit neighborhood. *(Ebony)*

Unfortunately, the church people disapproved of rhythm and blues, which led to the rather abrupt termination of Stevie's sojourn in the world of organized religion.

After school and on weekends, Stevie gave porch concerts. They were neither scheduled nor planned. It was simply that on a nice day, Stevie like to sit outside and sing and play his bongos or

his harmonica. An admirer of Ray Charles, he would copy the older man's singing style, and as he was so good at mimicry he would usually attract a small crowd of listeners. Responding to the attention, Stevie would entertain as long as anyone cared to listen. One day, one of the members of the Whitestone Baptist Church happened by and was shocked to find a member of the church choir not only singing "that music" but singing it right out on the street to boot. As Stevie recalls, "She said, 'Oh Stevie, I'm ashamed of you for playing that worldly music out here. I'm so ashamed of you.' Ha, I really blew it, boy. I'd been a junior deacon in the church and I used to sing solo at the services. But she went and told them what I was doing and they told me to leave. And that's how I became a sinner."

He would miss the gospel songs, and the guest singers who came to the church on important occasions. The church had been a happy, hopeful place where people expressed love in a way Stevie understood—through music. But if his relationship with the Whitestone Baptist Church came to a rather bitter end, it did not seriously affect him. His life was moving ahead. Disappointed by the attitude of the church, he changed his career plans. He had been thinking of becoming a minister; there were enough blind ministers to make this a realistic goal. Now he decided he would be a doctor, or an engineer.

Oddly enough, he did not at that time consider a career in music, but on he went making it, and listening to it. He recalls, "The kind of stuff I used to listen to was like . . . oh, like "Dream Lover," you know, and some Mary Wells stuff, "On Broadway," stuff like that. I liked the Five Royales, Johnny Ace, Clyde McPhatter, Jackie Wilson, Jimmy Reed, the Drifters. Oh, Jimmy Reed. Oh, I used to love that boy, I swear. Oh, the music! Jumping around and dancing . . . Do you remember that tune, what was it . . . 'da da da *da* da da da duh . . .' 'Honky Tonk!' *Bad!* Bill Doggett. Remember? And the Coasters, the Dixie Hummingbirds, the Staple Singers . . . ooooh, God! That Mavis Staples! I swear to God, I've been in love with that chick so long . . ."

And on he went learning to live as a blind person in a sighted world. He remembers, "I mostly had a sighted person with me so I was rarely put into situations where I was scared or would start to feel alone. I do remember one frightening thing, though. One time my father decided to take me out with him. I was pretty young—I must have been around seven or eight—he said to me, you want to go, Stevie, with me? We gonna go and get some candy and stuff, bubble gum and stuff . . . ride the bus and c'mon! And I said okay, you know, and I was jumping up and down and was excited about it and we went over to this house and he had a piano over there and a saxophone—I never knew what one looked like—and I stayed there for a while, we stayed together . . . and then one day I remember him having to go off somewhere and he stayed away for a long time—and left me alone. That was the first time I got upset and I started to cry about that. But after a while I just said, hey, forget it, and I just went to sleep. I was just afraid because the surroundings weren't familiar to me."

In familiar surroundings, as he tells it, "I used to get into a lot of shit, Jack! I got caught trying to mess with this girl. I was about eight years old. It was the playhouse trip. And I really was like taking the girl's clothes off and everything. I don't understand how I did that shit and everything. I don't understand how I did that stuff. I was *in* it! I had her in my room with my clothes off. And she gave it away 'cause she started laughin' and giggling 'cause I was touching her."

Back in his home neighborhood Stevie was a very popular child, not only because of the concerts, but because he was very outgoing, constantly alert for sounds and smells which would tell him things that maybe no one else would know. He would go to the store with his mother, and enjoy the world of voices and the mingled smells of food and detergents and soaps. For a sighted child a visit to a grocery store involves packages, cans with bright labels, the sight of food and vegetables. But for Stevie the grocery store was a magic world of sensation. His education, like that of any blind child, was something that took place as much out of school as in it. As much on the sidewalk as in the classroom. Learning to move around safely in a new apartment when the family moved to Detroit, learning the feel of new stairs in the project, new neighborhood, new streets. Identifying new people by sound, smell, touch—all this is a kind of special course which the blind must take all their lives. But when Stevie was nine, a new dimension was added to his life-course, a dimension that few people, young or old, blind or sighted, experience. Little Stevie Morris was signed to a recording contract.

Although he was blind, as a child Stevie did not feel all that different from other children. He played many of their games, compensating for his lack of sight with his other senses, and was in many ways "just one of the kids." *(Ebony)*

2

Stevie's Big Break

Most people have to comb the world to find the place, the time, the circumstances where they can make a start—not necessarily a place where they can succeed, just make a start, put a toe in the water. Stevie's start found him, when he was playing on a Detroit porch. Out of the church, no longer welcome in the choir, Stevie spent more and more time giving porch concerts, and every time he performed he was learning. Not only was he improving his musical skills, finding things he could do that he hadn't been able to do the week before, but learning how to handle an audience, learning how to reach out and carry them along with him on his music. All Stevie knew at the time was that playing and singing was what made him happier than anything else. That's why he did it, that's why it sounded so good, but he was learning all the same. One of his steady porch concert partners was John Glover, whose cousin Ronnie White was a member of the Miracles. The Miracles recorded for a black-owned Detroit company called Hitsville U.S.A. Every time he saw his famous cousin, little John Glover would boast about his friend

(Paul Slade, *Pictorial Parade*)

For Stevie, one of the nicest things about signing with Hitsville, U.S.A. was the opportunity he had to play all the instruments in the recording studio. He spent hours there each week. *(Ebony)*

(Ebony)

Stevie, the kid who lived in his block, who seemed to be able to do just about anything in music, the kid who had taught himself to play the harmonica, the piano, the drums. And Ronnie, not unnaturally, didn't pay much attention; he brushed little John aside in the way that grownups always do brush aside little kids who pester them about "My friend who . . ." Then one day when Ronnie was visiting his relatives the Glovers, Stevie just happened to be out there playing and singing, making music, enjoying himself. And such music it was that Ronnie stopped dead in his tracks and really listened. When one talented singer hears another talented singer performing, especially a nine-year-old out on the sidewalk, he has to do something about it. Ronnie knew that this kind of talent was rare indeed.

Ronnie introduced Stevie to Brian Holland, a writer for Hitsville, and Holland set up an audition for Stevie at Hitsville, taking him over there one afternoon, showing him the studios, letting him touch the instruments, the recording equipment, describing the scene for the little nine-year-old. The sounds, the textures, the smells of the new place he did not have to describe, for Stevie was all ears and nose, fingers touching instruments and equipment and telling him what they found, mind running at top speed. This was the place where he was to spend much of his life for the next eleven years.

After he had shown Stevie around, Brian Holland took him to see Berry Gordy, president of Hitsville. Stevie played the harmonica and the drums, and sang nonstop for forty-five minutes. By the time he had finished, Gordy was thinking about contract details.

Berry Gordy is a remarkable man, an acknowledged genius of the recording business. A former machinist for the Ford Motor Company, he had long been interested in music and had operated a publishing firm, Jobete, on the side. Jobete published all the material Gordy wrote for Marv Johnson, Jackie Wilson and others. In 1957 he also became an independent producer. From 1957 to 1959 he leased material by Marv Johnson to United Artists and by the Miracles to Chess. In 1959, his sister Anna formed her own label—Anna—in Detroit, and Gordy soon followed suit. Reportedly on $600 in borrowed money, he formed a small complex. Under an umbrella company called Hitsville U.S.A. were consolidated the Jobete Music Company and a label, Tammie, later changed to Tamla. Although Hitsville U.S.A. was renamed Motown, the publishing company, Jobete, still thrives as originally named, as does the Tamla label, although Gordy has tried issuing recordings on different labels, including Gordy, VIP and Soul.

It was a magnificent experiment, to say the least. At that time, blacks in the music business were almost exclusively in the performing sector. Very few held key positions in the administration of record companies. The few who did were primarily A&R directors of rhythm and blues music. Senior executives were exceedingly rare and owners almost nonexistent. A few black-owned companies had risen and fallen, a few others struggled along, but none were known outside the music industry. Berry Gordy's would be the first, and continues to be the most successful.

Gordy's nose for talent, his considerable business acumen, and his commercial instincts have all contributed to his success, but an important factor in those early days was less ascribable to any particular talent of Gordy's. Back in Detroit, in 1960, he was in the right place at the right time. New York, Philadelphia and Chicago all had major recording companies. Young black residents of those cities thus had an opportunity to be discovered by those companies and to graduate from amateur to professional status. Detroit, the nation's fourth largest black population center, had no major recording company, but it had just as high a percentage of talented black kids who were aware that music was their ticket out of the ghetto. Detroit was a virtual lode of musical gold. All that was needed was a smart entrepreneur to mine it, and Berry Gordy stepped in to fill that need.

All of Gordy's performers in the early years and many in the later years were local kids, and many were initially "discovered" by each other. Just as Ronnie White had discovered Stevie, the Supremes were brought to Gordy's attention by the Temptations, and Diana Ross discovered the Jackson Five.

But with Stevie, Berry Gordy was taking a more than average risk. A child performer is always more of a risk than an adult. There can be novelty value; a child with talent is appealing, charming, "cute." But how far can you go on cuteness, charm? Stevie was blind. Would that carry him further than the average child performer, or would that "novelty" too wear off with time? A child performer is an unstable commodity—he may make the tricky journey to adulthood and stay a top performer, and so be a long-term investment, or he may burn out around the time his voice changes. No one can tell for sure what will happen. But Berry Gordy took the risk, knowing that there had been many child stars who had fizzled out, many more failures than successes. Stevie might easily have gone nowhere.

Stevie was put under contract with Hitsville U.S.A. in 1960, at the age of nine. Because of the law that protects child performers from exploitation by unscrupulous adults, a court-appointed guardian was placed in charge of Stevie's affairs. His mother was given enough money to support the family and pay the rent, but the rest of his earnings, from the time when he signed with Hitsville at nine to the time when he reached twenty-one years of age, were put in trust for him. For all those years, although he was rich on paper, working very hard, he could not buy his mother a house, the first item on his list of gifts, nor could he buy himself musical instruments to play when he was home. (He made do with a tape recorder.) He was told, quite truthfully, that these restrictions were for his own protection, there had been child stars in the past who had worked their childhoods away only to find that there was no money after years of labor. Parents, agents, attorneys had managed to spend it all. But it was hard nonetheless. Stevie had been raised to be a giving person, and he dearly wanted to give to his family. He remembered the expeditions to pick up coal on a dry dock. Stevie knew that money meant warmth in winter, something better than beans for supper, some of the things the kids at school boasted about, and to have the money locked up until he was twenty-one must have seemed unfair.

Having satisfied the laws governing the finances of child performers, Hitsville had other laws by which to abide in Stevie's case. They would have to be careful that his work with them did not jeopardize his schooling, or violate child labor laws governing hours. They were more than willing to adhere to these regulations. And they were determined to do much more. In fact, in a rather cavalier manner, they proceeded to take over the task of raising little Steveland Morris. His tutor, Ted Hull, his music teacher, Mrs. Ardena Johnston, and his arranger, Clarence Paul, became like surrogate parents for him. Part of their job was to teach him the "right values." Hard work was rewarded, smoking and swearing were forbidden. The values of honesty and frugality were

preached to him constantly. He was given an allowance of $2.50 a week. Said Mrs. Johnston, "We hope to teach him to use his money wisely, to avoid champagne tastes."

Stevie, the child, was treated as a child at Hitsville, but he was not the only performer to feel the effects of Hitsville's *in loco parentis* attitude. The very nature of its personnel encouraged this situation—not just the fact that many of the performers were in their teens or that many had discovered each other but that several of Gordy's relatives held executive positions in the firm. But the key was Gordy himself. He kept a tight rein over his staff and his product, and he left nothing to chance. First, all his

The people at Hitsville were like a family to Stevie. They never forgot that he was still a little boy. Members of the company's public relations staff, his musical director, or his tutor could always find time to play a game with him or take him for a bicycle ride. (Paul Slade, *Pictorial Parade*)

performers were signed to exclusive contracts. Second, he contracted with several songwriters to write exclusively for him. Since the company was small, these writers were expected to do double-duty as producers. Although it is doubtful that the tendency for particular writing-producing teams to work regularly with particular performers was planned, it nevertheless came about, and in Gordy's view was good, since it enabled him to release records in a particular order. Although the artists had some input into the process, every phase of their work, whether recording or performing, was relatively controlled. In 1969, Stevie's music director was Gene Kee. "Tamla has a complete service for their artists," he explained. "The artist development people look after everything from buying their clothes to getting them to the job on time. You have to select material for the artist, cut the act and sharpen it up depending on where they are playing, check the choreography and generally act objectively for the artist." Essentially the same mode of operation had obtained from the very beginning. Some of the company's artists resented this control, among them Mary Wells and Kim Weston, but Stevie was too young to think about artistic independence. All he knew was that suddenly a whole new world had opened up to him.

In the early Hitsville days, when he was still living at home with his family and attending public school in Detroit, Stevie would go straight to the studio after school and hang around. He would have moved in altogether if he'd been allowed to. Clarence Paul, Stevie's first conductor at the company, says, "He was a pest. He'd come by at three every day after school and stay until dark. He'd play every instrument in the place and bust in on you when you was cuttin' somebody." (Stevie couldn't see when the red recording light was on.) But he was allowed his explorations. The people at Hitsville understood his need to make sounds and to be given free reign in exploring the new possibilities the company's recording studios presented. Studio drummer Benny Benjamin took a particular interest in him and taught him new drumming techniques. "I learned from just listening to him," Stevie recalls. Other performers and staff members treated him like a company mascot. Of course, he was far more, but although Gordy had an investment in the little boy, he did not rush to recoup it. Stevie was given the chance to become comfortable in his new surroundings. Almost a year passed before his first record was released.

Originally titled "You Made a Vow," it was issued under the title "Mother Thank You." It was an obvious attempt to exploit the human interest qualities of little Steveland Morris—the small blind boy with the sweet voice. It did not sell particularly well, and was hardly noticed outside the black urban music world. But the company was not greatly concerned by this lack of success. Stevie was being groomed, and it was understood that he needed recording experience before he could be expected to be a recording success. The lack of sales of his first record concerned Stevie not at all. He was so pleased to have had a record released that whether anyone other than his family and friends bought it was of minor importance. He had not yet begun to think of music as a career, with all its financial and business aspects; to him, making music was the thing, and given the unchecked opportunity to do so, he could not see beyond it.

Stevie's next record for Hitsville, released under the company's label, Tamla Records, was "I Call It Pretty Music." It did not make the charts either, but it sold better than "Mother Thank You." So did his next, "Contract on Love." By this time, Stevie had begun to develop a small following among black teenagers in the nation's large cities where Hitsville performers appeared. He may have been a minor act in the Hitsville shows, but the shows were so memorable that anyone connected with them benefited.

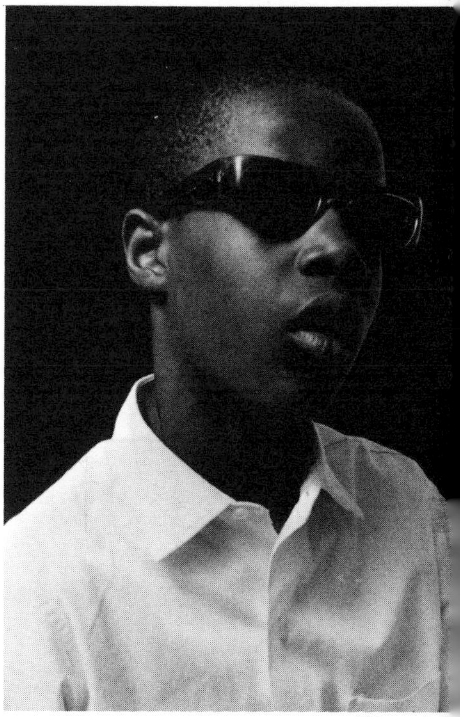
(Ebony)

Hitsville U.S.A. was still a struggling company. Black performers like Mary Wells, the Miracles and Martha and the Vandellas were still restricted to performing at theaters and auditoriums in black ghettos. But anyone attending one of their shows would have thought that Hitsville was grossing millions per annum and that the acts were doing a benefit on leave from the Copacabana in New York or the Los Angeles Civic Center. Even when he could ill afford it, Berry Gordy made substantial investments in costuming and choreography for his acts before he sent them out on the road. They might be going out to play before auditoriums and theaters filled with adolescents in dingy ghetto sections, but their acts would have all the glitter and polish of a spot on the "Ed Sullivan Show." This fact was not lost on their audiences, who showed their appreciation by spending their meager finances on Hitsville singles and albums. But these audiences would not have packed the auditoriums and theaters, nor purchased the records, had the Hitsville acts been little more

Stevie had a way with fans from the beginning. He loved signing autographs and practiced his signature so he could write well for the fans. *(Ebony)*

Right: **Stevie was a born performer, happiest when he was before an audience communicating with them through his music.** (Paul Slade, *Pictorial Parade*)

than glamour and sophistication. Slick presentation cannot overshadow a lack of caring for the audience, and in the case of Hitsville performers it was not called upon to do so. They piled off their buses and picked their way through garbage-strewn streets into cramped and dingy dressing rooms, and thirty minutes later emerged onto the stage dressed to the nines and positively glowing with the joy of performing. Perhaps it was because every single one of them had, not so many years before, been just like the adoring adolescents who stared up at them. All the early Hitsville performers had come from the streets of Detroit, and they had not forgotten how incredibly lucky they were to be up on that stage in

those fine clothes, getting the chance to perform. They loved it, and their audiences caught that feeling and enjoyed the show all the more because they were part of that enjoyment.

No one loved performing more than Stevie. A minor act he might have been, but he made the most of every moment of his comparatively brief appearances on stage. Dressed in his glittery suit, his head lolling from side to side, his foot tapping to the beat, he sang smiling; although the next show might be only two hours away he performed as if he would never get the chance again. Then he would be led into the wings and the Supremes or some other better-known act would come onstage; but when the show was over and the black ghetto kids who for a brief time had been transported out of their poverty and hopelessness and into the glamour of a Hitsville show excitedly recalled the various acts, they would remember the little blind kid who had performed like he was born to the stage, and they would go to the record stores and ask for his recordings.

So Stevie's career in the entertainment world began. And Hitsville became his second family. He did regular road trips with the Hitsville Revue, performing with other Hitsville stars in black theaters. But despite the acclaim of audiences, the support of the Hitsville management, and the company of his fellow performers, it was a lonely life. Removed from the close world of family and friends and neighborhood, he now found himself with adults, whether on the road or at the studio. His life as a performer separated him from his friends and from the other kids at school. Although he was hardly a nationally recognized star, his singles and albums were quite big in the Detroit area, and there were often autograph seekers waiting for him when he arrived at school. The other kids were suspicious of his success, jealous of him. "Stevie has changed," "Stevie's forgotten his old friends," they said.

It was not so, but the fact that the other kids believed he was different was enough to make him unhappy. He did not know how to convince them that he was just the same. Actually, although he thought he was the same, he was not. The wheels of life had spun faster for Stevie than they had for his schoolmates, and it is understandable that the other kids resented the fact that he might have a destiny that was denied to them. The general feeling was that Stevie would be brought to his senses sooner or later, cut down to size.

Many of his teachers seemed to share that feeling, but they were merely voicing the attitude of the system for which they worked and of which they were a part. A school system is a bureaucracy, and it delivers education to the blind, as to other children, along very narrow lines. In order to function efficiently, the Detroit public school system had had to decide exactly what the average blind child could and could not do, which aspirations were safe and which were not. The bureaucracy did not function at the level of teaching its handicapped students to be really successful, yet here was a blind student being successful in a way nobody in authority had planned for him. Suppose all blind students decided to take off on road trips and perform in theaters for money, were acclaimed by audiences, cut records, signed autographs? The system could not handle the presence of a young blind star, and after considerable hemming and hawing, announced that Stevie could not be educated properly if he was always going on tours and therefore would no longer be allowed to tour. Stevie remembers that "when the Board of Education said I couldn't perform, that the Detroit schools couldn't accommodate my wanting to go on the road, I cried and I cried and prayed for a long time."

(Paul Slade, *Pictorial Parade*)

Children are always at the mercy of adults, blind children that much more so, and Stevie was not unreasonable in fearing that they would somehow stop him from making music, that this marvelous new existence that had made him so happy might come to an end. Despite assurances from Hitsville that something would be worked out, he was afraid, and the wait for a final decision to be made about his future was agonizing. At last a school superintendent with imagination suggested Stevie be enrolled in a private institution, the Michigan School for the Blind at Lansing. There, the curriculum was more flexible, and the bureaucracy much more manageable; it would be able to cope with Stevie's frequent absences and would allow them, provided he was accompanied by a private tutor while on the road.

Although enrolling at the Michigan School for the Blind seemed to represent the answer to Stevie's problems, it would also represent yet another wedge between him and any semblance of a normal life. It would mean leaving his home and family, for Lansing was 150 miles away from Detroit, and there would be little time for visits home. Given the age range of Hitsville's prime audience, school vacations were excellent times for road trips. In this regard,

Stevie's mother proved herself a remarkable woman. She did not relish the prospect of her third and most vulnerable son's being so far away from his family and familiar surroundings. But she realized if she vetoed the idea of his attending the Michigan School for the Blind she would be depriving him of his chance to do what he loved best. So she swallowed her need, and chose to respect his, a choice that may have been the second most important event in Stevie's early career. For if Stevie had not been fortunate enough to have gotten on a collision course with the Detroit Board of Education, he might never have been forced really to study music at all.

At his new school, his blind music teacher was determined to introduce Stevie to the works of Chopin and Bach, and insisted that he concentrate on their kind of music. If he grumbled at times, complained about the dull, old-fashioned music, he was learning in spite of himself, and this classical education proved invaluable for Stevie's future. With his natural ability for music, he had picked up much already, but the right music teacher could help him develop a firm technique to build on. And since he was to go on to write his own music, studying the formal structures of classical composers gave him the mechanics to deal with his own imagination, a technical background that would serve him well. One of the most important things for an artist is not to be limited technically, to be able to reach out for what he needs. Although people sometimes think technique and imagination are two separate entities, they really are part and parcel of the same thing. A good technique is the means to expressing what lies in the heart and mind, the machinery with which the imagination can be made visible, or rather audible. Gradually, Stevie's ear overcame his mental prejudices. What sounded initially like alien chords and tonal structures began to make sense to him, and he saw their possibilities. When he was twelve years old, Stevie composed two concertos. When he played them for his conductor Clarence Paul, and others at Hitsville, they started calling him the little boy wonder.

As a professional, Stevie met other music professionals, like the late singer Bobby Darin. They all admired his talent as a musician and did not mind his special way of meeting them. (Paul Slade, *Pictorial Parade*)

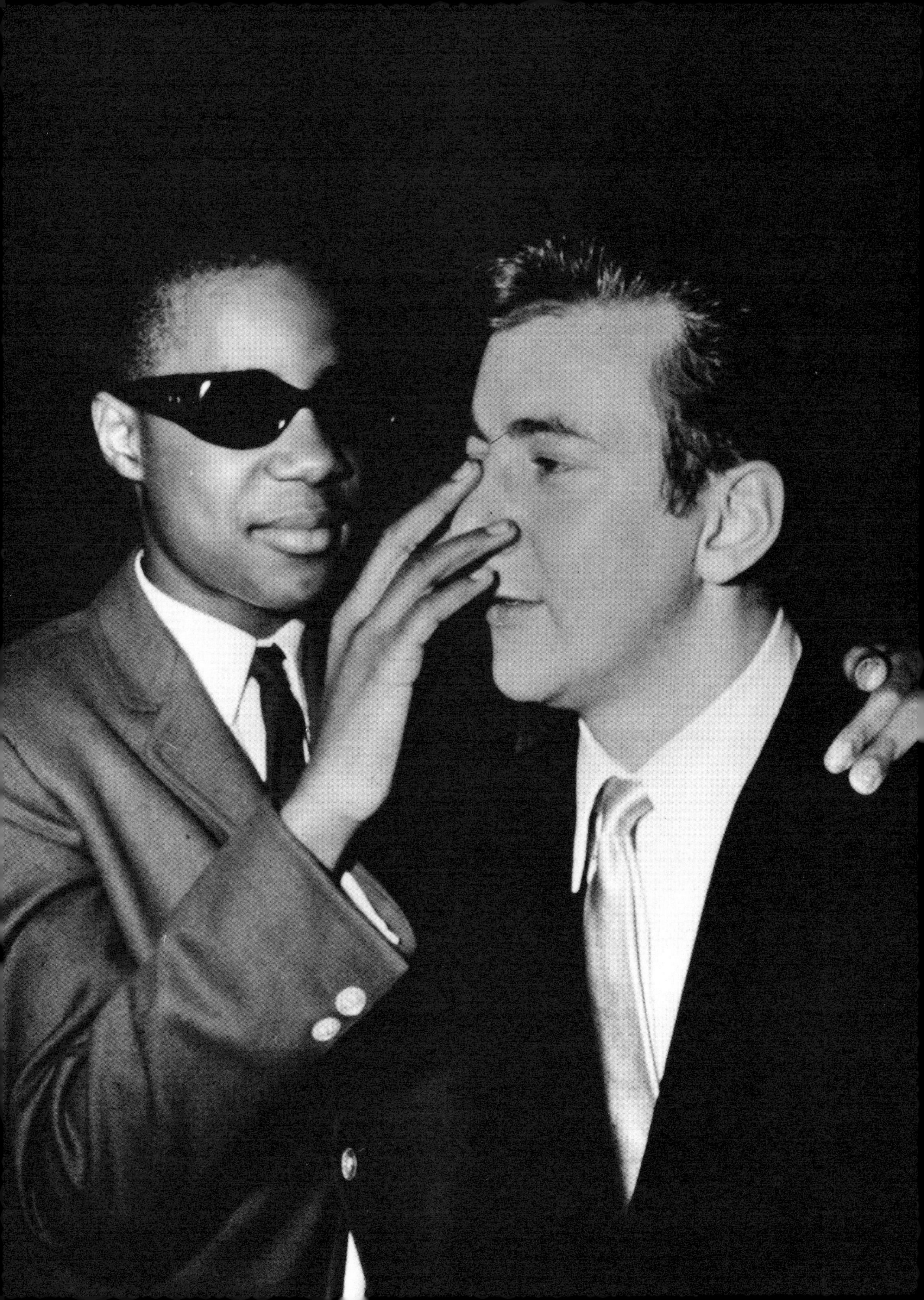

3

Little Stevie Wonder

(United Press International)

Even people who considered Stevie a mere child star recognized his talent as a musician when they heard him play the harmonica. *(Globe Photos)*

Stevie made it big when he was thirteen years old, interestingly with a record that was not entirely in the Hitsville style. Most of the Hitsville artists under contract were vocalists, and the company's "sound" showed a strong influence of church singing, leaning more heavily on gospel at that time. Stevie's first two records had been of that mold. But Stevie spent so much time around the Hitsville studios that the people there could not help noticing his own, individual style. When left on his own he was far more likely to concentrate on instrumentation—on the drums or the harmonica or one of the countless other instruments he was learning to master—and to vocalize not actual lyrics but various "riffs": "do, do, do," or "lah, la, la" or "yeah, yeah, yeah." One day it occurred to somebody that maybe Stevie ought to be allowed to make a recording in this, his own natural style. Having noticed the incredible energy he put into his on-stage performances—he had made history at New York's Apollo Theatre at the age of twelve wailing in front of a seventeen-piece band and bringing the house down—the people at Hitsville made another smart move: they decided to let him record before a live audience. The result was "Fingertips."

The people at Hitsville were excited about the record, and they felt Stevie should have an exciting name to go with it. His musical director, Clarence Paul, called him Little Stevie. Others often referred to him as the little boy wonder. Someone suggested combining the two: Little Stevie Wonder was the result. Says Stevie: "I personally liked my real name better." For publicity purposes, the title was extended, and he became "Little Stevie Wonder, the Twelve-Year-Old Genius." Since the record was not released until June of 1963, Stevie was actually thirteen, and when you're thirteen you don't like everyone thinking you're only twelve. But no matter—otherwise the record was all true Stevie.

"Fingertips" was a novelty, a rhythm and blues shouter, performed by a flashy little bopper with perfect control, control of the wild screeching harmonica, control of his voice. The tune had no lyrics as such, although the vocalizing showed the current influence of gospel call-and-response in Hitsville music. It consisted of Stevie singing "Yeah, yeah, yeah." But Stevie had a way of singing "Yeah, yeah, yeah" that was different from the way anyone else had ever done it. He would later have similar success with other "riffs," notably "La, la, la, la, la, la" and "Do do wop." Both were infectious, and the inclusion of the live audience reaction was an inspiration. But what sold the record, what brought listeners and other live audiences to their feet was the wild, innocent joy of Stevie Wonder, the little blind boy joyfully showing off to the world what he could do.

"Fingertips" reached a new audience. It moved out of Detroit to Philadelphia, where Dick Clark's "American Bandstand" had caught on in a way that even the show's own producers found incredible. Millions of white teenagers were introduced to black urban rhythm and blues music on "American Bandstand," and millions heard the name Stevie Wonder for the first time via the same vehicle. "Fingertips" screeched to the top of the singles charts and stayed there for fifteen weeks. Stevie Wonder was suddenly a nationally known name, and in August of that year he received the first of many accolades. *Billboard* magazine named him the Number One Artist in the Nation. The award, was translated into braille for Stevie and it remains one of his prized possessions.

"Fingertips" also put Berry Gordy's company on its feet, once and for all, and perhaps in consideration of being "on the music map," the company's name was changed to Motown. This is not to say that Hitsville/Motown would not have made it without Stevie Wonder. The white teenage audience was beginning to accept the black R&B sound, and Gordy certainly had the talent to capitalize on the trend. Three years earlier, "Shop Around" by Smokey Robinson and the Miracles had become the first Hitsville release to reach the top ten in the singles charts and since then the company had one single in the top ten each year. But "Fingertips" reached Number One, and it stayed there for fifteen weeks. It was the first of many "firsts" that Stevie amassed for Motown. He was their first star to tour overseas in England, France, Japan, the first to tour in the States with the increasingly popular English group, the Rolling Stones. The first to appear in motion pictures, *Muscle Beach Party*. The first to appear on network television, "Ed Sullivan," "Mike Douglas," "American Bandstand," "Where the Action Is," "Tom Jones."

(United Press International)

It wasn't only the sales of over one million copies, but the fact that this success showed the music business as a whole that Berry Gordy's nose for talent was remarkable. "Fingertips" did a lot of things for a lot of people. It established both the child prodigy and the corporation. Still, even during its weeks as Number One on the charts, everyone in the business knew it was a novelty; a twelve-year-old prepubescent blind harmonica player and a live audience that undoubtedly helped draw the maximum performance from Stevie. It is one thing to perform in a theater in front of an audience and another to cut in a studio. The question was, could the novelty be made to work again?

In the meantime, there was no point in not capitalizing on the novelty for as long as possible. A few months later, Motown issued Stevie's album, "The Twelve-Year-Old Genius," which was almost assured of success because it contained "Fingertips." In fact, Stevie set a precedent in the record industry when the single and the album were simultaneously in the Number One positions on the charts for several weeks. Stevie did even more road shows to publicize both the single and the album, and now he was not just a minor act. He was the star.

He was doing what he wanted to do most in the world—perform—yet in order to do it he had to put up with extreme emotional isolation. There were constantly people around him, on tour, at the studios, at school, yet he was very alone.

Hitsville ran its child star's life according to a rigid schedule—scheduled concerts, scheduled homework, scheduled bedtimes, scheduled recording sessions. The telephone became his lifeline to those he loved, and it remains one of the most important instruments in his life. Today, he likes to carry on as many as six different conversations simultaneously and he is rarely far away from a telephone. Deprived of a comfortable, secure, ever-present family life, he turned even more to his inner self and his rich fantasy life. It was an intense, interior world, as are those of all blind persons, and the blind are always under pressure from living it. The very interior quality of Stevie's world has added a dimension of feeling to his music. His love of the audience is both the love of the great performer and a necessary outlet for his emotions. An audience gives him an opportunity to say many things whose expression would otherwise be denied him by his blindness, and also allows him to release that frantic energy that is the source of his "blindisms," the lolling of his head and the twisting of his body that would put off American television producers as he grew older.

"When *I* look at an audience, all I see are beautiful people," says Stevie, but it is not his blindness that makes him such an outstanding performer. It seems he was born with the gift, and it is hard to imagine that such talent would not have come to the surface sooner or later. Even as a child star, he often became so involved with the audience that he would ignore the fact that his number was over and it was exit time. He would ignore the frantic whispers from backstage. "I used to pick him up and carry him off," Clarence Paul remembers. But the fact is that poverty buries thousands of people with talent, whose energies are spent instead on survival and whose aspirations never have a chance to make it to the surface. If Ronnie White had not happened by that day, when Stevie was giving one of his porch concerts, he might still be giving sidewalk concerts to people sitting on their porches in the Detroit ghetto. He might have remained Steve Morris, "that blind guy who's better than some of those people you see on TV." Despite the loneliness, the long separations from his family, the rigidity of the Hitsville child-raising formula, Stevie realized that he owed his opportunities to perform to Motown, and he was grateful. He said once when he was thirteen, "I was just another

little blind boy before I came to Hitsville. That was the best thing that ever happened to me." But he could not spend the rest of his life performing "Fingertips."

It is the bane of every successful artist's life. After the big one that makes the artist a name, what next? Do you capitalize on the success and risk repeating yourself, certain death artistically? Do you strike out in a new direction? If you decide to, will the audience go with you? Or will they complain because you've done something different from what they expected? Will they fail to buy? Will they act hurt? "We expected more of him than that." The world is fickle, and audiences are *very* fickle. The adults in Stevie's life were aware of these considerations, of the uncertainty of Stevie's continued career. What would happen to him if he didn't make it? There were people hanging in the wings, waiting for the young musician to fail, who would say "I told you so," happy that he had failed.

Following the success of *Fingertips*, at the age of thirteen, Stevie went on his first tour abroad. He appeared in a show at the Olympia Music Hall in Paris with British teenage singer Louise Cordet. *(Wide World Photos)*

(Paul Slade, *Pictorial Parade*)

The problem was that no one yet knew how to classify Little Stevie Wonder, and though his natural style had been acknowledged in "Fingertips," he was not considered old enough to classify himself. He had a range of talents, particularly instrumental. Some people at Motown were drawn to the idea that, as a blind, black, talented instrumentalist and vocalist, he was destined to inherit the mantle that Ray Charles would someday pass on to a suitable heir, and so Stevie recorded an album called "Tribute to Uncle Ray." The album enjoyed only modest sales. Perhaps Little Stevie Wonder was too much of an original to be a young understudy. So "The Jazz Soul of Little Stevie" was issued. Emphasizing his talent on drums, it, too, enjoyed only modest sales.

Stevie, meanwhile, was largely unaware of this corporate concern over his musical future. He was still so wrapped up in his inner musical world and its counterpart, live performing, that he could not look ahead, indeed had no reason to. The release of a new album did not mean, to him, a foray into the harsh world of critical reviews and sales figures in the red or in the black. Instead, it meant little more than an increase in attention. For days before "The Jazz Soul of Little Stevie" was released, he practiced signing his name, knowing that all the secretaries and technicians would want autographed copies and members of the press would probably be around to record the moment. After autographing a copy for Berry Gordy, he announced happily, "This is the very best signature I have ever seen." Stevie's forte was not just performing onstage; he did a pretty good job for the publicity people as well.

But albums sell because singles sell, usually, not the other way around. Stevie needed a new hit single. More harmonica novelty numbers were tried, but "Workout Stevie, Workout," issued in October 1963, reached only the thirty-third position on the charts, and "Hey Harmonica Man" (June 1964) did only slightly better, reaching number twenty-nine. "Castles in the Sand," (February 1964) never got higher than the fifty-second position. By 1965, the people at Motown were forced to conclude that they still had not found the right vehicle for Little Stevie Wonder. Meanwhile, the "Motown Sound" was catching on. From 1963 on, the emphasis had been shifting from church singing to the qualities of gospel. Accordingly, the musical arrangements had also been changed.

As Charlie Gillett explains in his book *The Sound of the City:*

> "Tambourines, clapping, a steady four-even beats-to-the-bar rhythm, call-and-response harmony structure, advisory and moralizing songs were all introduced or exaggerated, and by 1965 the sound was fully conceived. More imaginatively than anyone had done before, Gordy and his co-producers had translated the qualities of church music into popular music terms, and yet retained, even enhanced, the excitement and conviction of the religious singers, while staisfying the need for a more sophisticated sound."

At Motown, this "sound" practically became a system. It would be criticized by many as "processed soul," and indeed some of the records produced in the mid-sixties merited such criticism, although others can be counted as some of the best of their time. By 1965, Smokey Robinson and the Miracles had come up with two hits, "You Really Got a Hold on Me" (1963) and "The Tracks of My Tears" (1965). The Supremes had come along in 1964 and been an instant sensation with "Baby Love." After getting one single in the top ten in 1960 and 1961, Gordy's company had sported four in 1962, six in 1963 and five in 1964. The feeling was that it was time for a Motown formula recording for Little Stevie Wonder, and in August 1965, "High-Heeled Sneakers" was issued. Unfortunately, it did not take off, but saw only a modest, eight-week stay in the number fifty-nine position on the charts. At Motown, some intensive analysis was called for. The analysts looked at Stevie's performance and found nothing wanting. They concluded, then, that it had been the song itself—not the beat or the rhythm but the lyrics. Although the term was not in use at the time, had the Motown analysts possessed linguistic foreknowledge, they would have concluded that the song might be a little too "ethnic"; a little too hard for the white teenage audience to relate to. After all, how many white teenages were familiar with women wearing "wig hats" on their heads? And even the red dress might be a bit too flashy for general consumption. It was not Stevie, but the song, they concluded, so in a short time a new Stevie Wonder song was issued. "Up Tight (Everything's All Right)" was released in January 1966.

Almost immediately, it climbed to number three on the charts, and it stayed there for fourteen weeks, almost equalling the tenacity and the popularity of "Fingertips." It proved Stevie Wonder was not just a novelty, but it proved much more. It established him as a vocalist; the harmonica was not featured at all in "Up Tight." "I talked this over with my musical director, Clarence Paul," said Stevie a few weeks later, "and we figured that 'Up Tight' didn't need harp. Vocal is much stronger on such a number." It also established him as a songwriter. For the first time, his name, S. Judkins, was listed in the writers' credits, along with co-authors Sylvia Moy and Henry Cosby. One critic noticed the credit to "S. Judkins" and wondered about it, only one of many people who would inquire about the different names by which Stevie Wonder has been known. It presents a particular headache to music and music publication indexers. The Music Index lists him this way: "Stevie Wonder (r.n. Stephen D. Judkins or Steveland Morris or Steveland Judkins Hardaway)." Stevie explains, "Judkins is my father's name. But it's crazy to explain it. Morris was on my birth certificate and everything, but Judkins was my father. I took his name when I was in school. We just signed the song contract like that." The problem is not only with his last name. Steve signs his name "Stevland."

Although critics didn't find "Up Tight" very interesting in content, a Motown formula song, nonetheless it was an excellent vehicle for Stevie's voice. It was partly a question of the fact that being blind, Stevie had to express everything through his voice and his playing. Quite ordinary "packaged" emotions became much more intense when he sang a song that another singer would have made banal. "A Place in the Sun," "Shoo-Be-Doo-Be-Doo-Da-Day," "Yester-Me, Yester-You, Yesterday," "For Once in My Life," "My Cherie Amour"—after —"Up Tight" in 1966, Stevie's credit began to appear on most of the songs he performed. Slowly, he was beginning to take charge.

Stevie had written two concertos when he was twelve, and he had been writing ever since. Like so many other performers, he had found writing music the way he wanted it to be was a natural follow-up to his playing and singing, an extra and essential dimension for the complete musical experience. Motown had a glossy sound, good to dance to, upbeat, slick rhythm and blues, a clear beat. Stevie had learned the system, learned the ins and outs of the sound, what worked and what didn't. But he had kept to his own way of thinking. There was a strong streak of independence in

Stevie, and the streak would grow wider and deeper with the passing years. Even in the slickest of his early songs, he would inject a little something that wasn't anyone but Stevie himself. For his contribution to "Up Tight," he freely gave credit to the influence of the Rolling Stones and their record "Satisfaction." "Satisfaction" had been a big hit in the United States. On tour with the Stones in 1964, Stevie had observed how audiences had reacted to it. He had liked the sound and seen no reason not to use the elements in it that appealed to other American listeners. As he explained to a British interviewer a few weeks later, "At the moment, everything in the U.S. is 'A Go Go.' It's the new world. It means anything that involves some sort of action, or movement. If someone thinks a record is good they might say, 'It's a go-go record,' y' know?"

His influences were many, he would explain. He dug Ray Charles—"He's my idol"—but he also liked Neil Sedaka and Stan Getz and even some avant garde material, "but I can't stand this feedback stuff!" He never exactly lauded the Motown sound, but he never put it down either. By the time "Up Tight" was issued critics in the business had taken to identifying the Motown formula in none too positive terms, notwithstanding the fact that a lot of other recording companies at the time would have given their eyeteeth to have been able to copy it. "Motown has a distinctive sound," Stevie would say, "and it is a sound that just about everybody has tried to copy but not been able to. I think that the distinctive sound has something to do with the acoustics in the studios at Detroit." He would continue, "I realize that there is quite a bit of similarity between Tamla/Motown records, but the guys at Motown realize this and they are beginning to change it." This is a fifteen-year-old talking! But Stevie Wonder was not your ordinary fifteen-year-old. This was a kid who would tour Britain and give a new word (uptight) to London's hip talk, who could command an audience like a veteran, who could look a growing and increasingly powerful corporation in the eye and insist on a measure of musical independence.

As soon as "Up Tight" became successful, Motown decided to capitalize on it. Two more Stevie Wonder singles were released in relatively rapid succession, "Nothing's Too Good for My Baby" (April 23, 1966) and "With a Child's Heart" (June 25, 1966). They represented a compromise between artist and corporation, the

By the age of seventeen, Stevie was appearing in costumes more appropriate to his age and sporting just a hint of a moustache. Musically, he was mature far beyond his years.
(United Press International)

first being a standard that Stevie liked, the second a new song that the people at Motown liked. Neither proved decisively the argument of either side. "Nothing's Too Good for My Baby" reached the number four spot on the charts and remained there for eleven weeks. "With a Child's Heart" was on the charts for eight weeks and reached the number eight position. Stevie, for one, remained undaunted. Back in January 1966 he had predicted that pretty songs would come back, and he still believed they would. The fact that the two singles had not been great successes only meant that the time for such songs had not yet come. He was also sufficiently satisfied with the performance of "Nothing's Too Good for My Baby" to stick solidly by his contention that he could render the songs of others and still sell records. In fact, he had it in his head to record "Blowin' in the Wind."

When they heard that, the people at Motown were dismayed. The Motown sound was something you could dance to, and you couldn't dance to that type of number. Why, it had already been successfully recorded by folk singers Peter, Paul and Mary and had been established as a folk song. But it had been clear very early on that the little boy wonder was no Motown cipher. "I never felt that I strictly embodied the Motown sound," Stevie says. "I mean there weren't too many people around there doing white folk stuff like 'Blowin' in the Wind' or 'Mr. Tambourine Man' like I was." In Stevie's mind, if a song moved him, that was enough, because whether he had written it himself, or whether it had been written and performed by someone else, he knew he would bring himself to it. And when he could do that, he knew that he would give the song a feeling that no one else in the world could give it. Perhaps he thought of the piano teacher at the Michigan School for the Blind, who had found things in Bach and Chopin to which his young, blind student could relate and to which he had given his own special feeling. Stevie felt that a song was a song, a public entity that he should be able to interpret if he wanted to, especially if he could make his interpretation special.

A friend of the author, Rochelle Larkin, remembers Stevie singing "Blowin' in the Wind":

"He sang it at a concert that was a complete bomb," she says. "Outdoors, in an enormous baseball field, horrible acoustics, cold and rainy. By the end of the first half, everyone, including the promoters, wished they'd stayed home. Toward the end of the second half, Stevie Wonder came out and sang 'Blowin' in the Wind' as if that song had never been sung before. Suddenly he wasn't 'Little' Stevie Wonder any more. He came out of the child-entertainer, novelty category and brought the crowd to its feet. He had reached for something and had caught it, and there was no longer a boy Wonder, but a man."

Stevie had his way at Motown, and his recording of "Blowin' in the Wind," released in July of 1966, reached number nine on the singles charts and stayed there for ten weeks. The critics dubbed it "soupy," but the fans bought it. He followed that success five months later with "A Place in the Sun," which also reached number nine.

Stevie just kept on expanding his musical horizons. Still attending the Michigan School for the Blind, he was also taking extension courses in composing and arranging at the University of California, and he was exercising his new knowledge by writing more and more songs. "I love writing so much," he told a reporter in London. "I go to places like London or Paris and it's fantastic understanding people and atmospheres. They help me to write songs, too. Different atmospheres inspire songs in me and maybe something happens to me while I'm abroad—I'll put that into a song, or maybe a song about my thoughts about that happening." He carried his tape recorder wherever he went, keeping it handy so when a snatch of melody, a catchy "riff," or the beginning of a lyric came into his head, he could record it. On the rare weekends he spent at home, he put these elements together into songs, and on one such weekend he and his mother got together and in approximately ten minutes came up with "I Was Made to Love Her."

(Wide World Photos)

Like most of Stevie's songs, it was autobiographical. "It is the feeling of a girl," he would explain. "We grew up together and we've made it through the years. People have disagreed with us and tried to get in the way and though mountains may crumble we'll still make it." He wrote the melody and chord structures, but his mother made important contributions. "She came up with the phrases," he happily acknowledged. "It was the first time she worked on a song with me. It really delighted her. She used to be a gospel singer." Released in June of 1967, "I Was Made to Love Her" more than recouped the losses on two previous, poorly performing singles, "Travlin' Man" and "Hey Love." It held the number two spot on the singles charts for fifteen weeks, during which time Stevie set off on an exhausting touring schedule.

It was the first time Gene Kee had accompanied Stevie on tour. Kee had joined Motown in February 1967 and had worked at first with several other artists and groups—the Supremes, the Spinners, Jimmy Ruffin and Marvin Gaye—as well as casually with Stevie. During the tour, he marveled at Stevie's calmness and poise. "It was hectic," he recalls, "a seven-day tour doing several shows a day and he had his schooling schedule as well as recording. But there were no hangups. I was concerned about how it was going to affect him but he has the temperament. He came through." Kee had cause to marvel again when later in the year Stevie set off on yet another tour of Britain, where "I Was Made to Love Her" was also high on the charts. During that tour, Stevie had an infection in his vocal chords that prevented him from singing in a high register. But the infection seemed to daunt him not at all. He was his smiling, finger-popping, energetic self, and he played to packed audiences wherever he went.

His career continued to soar. In the next two years, interspersed with a few less than memorable singles, he recorded "Shoo-Be-Doo-Be-Doo-Da-Day," "For Once in My Life," and "My Cherie Amour." Each reached the top ten on the singles charts. With each, his skill at playing his voice like a musical instrument increased, as did his skill at songwriting. "My Cherie Amour," which he wrote in thirty minutes, was, in his opinion, musically the best thing he had ever written. Interestingly, it was the B side of "I Don't Know Why," which never got higher than thirty-ninth spot on the charts.

Not everyone thought much either of his voice or of his lyric-writing ability. "Wonder definitely does not have a wonderful voice," wrote a critic in a *Variety* review of Stevie's performance at Marty's on Hill in New York. "In fact, his high-pitch shrill sounds can create a disturbing effect on the ears. But his cult of many fans see it differently. They were with the now maturing Detroiter all the way, applauding his every move, in tune with his every sound. It mattered little what the semi-audible lyrics had to say, what he did with his intense desire to please was more important."

"For Once in My Life" was a gold record in the United States and did very well in Britain, occasioning yet another British tour, this time with two other Motown groups, the Foundations and the Flirtations. The show, however, was mostly Stevie and Stevie was a quintessential performer. He commanded the stage, and the audience, and it was easy to forget that he was blind. But Stevie, and the Motown people who accompanied him on tour, never did. Because he was blind his performances were planned and rehearsed in even greater detail than those of other performers. The microphone, for example, had to be placed at a specific spot on the stage, and Stevie's entrance rehearsed so when it was his turn to go on he could walk directly to the mike. Some years before, at a big rock concert, someone had inadvertently moved the microphone. "I almost fell into the orchestra pit trying to find it," Stevie recalls, laughing. At the time, however, it was no laughing matter, and great pains were taken to see that the incident was not repeated. It is amazing that Stevie has never seriously injured himself in an onstage accident, for when he performs he is constantly in motion. The same *Variety* reviewer who had criticized his voice and his material had been frankly admiring of his onstage presence: "He is a super salesman who has developed the art of timing in compounding his multi-talents into something which is a show in the truest sense of the word. He gets loud and growling, but he knows when to soften up via the mouth organ. If he isn't hopping, laughing and clapping, he is curling the notes to the point of making it a real, old-fashioned revival 'soul' meeting. To put it midly, he is the essence of animation."

Opening with a rendition of Bobby Hebb's "Sunny," he would move into a harmonica solo, frequently "Alfie," then swing into "Shoo-Be-Doo-Be-Doo-Da-Day." On to the drums, which never failed to bring the audience to their feet. He played his audiences like instruments as well. Having excited them with his raucous but controlled drumming, he would quiet them with a ballad like Jim Webb's "By the Time I Get to Phoenix," then build their excitement with his latest hit single before ending with an older hit. He paced the show to perfection. He would leave the audience cheering, stomping, and shouting for more. He loved being in Britain. "I like the people here very much," he told a reporter. "They're so relaxed. In that sense, there's a similarity between the people here and in Japan." He did not say it, but he was comparing the atmosphere in Britain to that back home, and the atmosphere back home was hardly relaxed.

Back home, the nation was in the throes of the sixties. He was protected from the effects of racism in a personal sense, but the undercurrents were too strong for anyone to miss. There were the riots in Watts and Detroit following Martin Luther King's assassination, the turmoil of the decade which brought America face to face with itself. At home, the civil rights movement was bringing the injustices, the mistreatment of black Americans to the forefront of the news, and causing not only whites but blacks too to rethink what America was truly about. There was the war in Asia consuming so many lives each year, and so many lives of the poor, whites, blacks and other minorities, people without the education or the resources to evade the draft. It was the time of national identity crisis, and it took place when Stevie was in his teens, wondering as all teenagers do who and what he was, what the future held.

Although he was a veteran performer and musician by the age of seventeen, Stevie was still just a kid, eager to please and not very sophisticated outside the world of music. *(United Press International)*

4

Stevie Wonder Grows Up

He was no longer Little Stevie Wonder. He was eighteen years old, over six feet tall and shaving. Soon, he would sport a moustache in recognition of his adulthood, and perhaps in an attempt to make Motown recognize he was not a child anymore.

Stevie was almost a man, and he was tired of the Motown strictures. Soon he would be twenty-one, and he was thinking of striking out on his own. *(Wide World Photos)*

As with every other growing kid in the world, the scheduled life of school, work, work, school rankled more with every passing year. Every growing kid wants the same allowance, the same clothes, the same everything as other kids of his age. But Stevie wasn't the same as other kids. Blindness cut him off from the ordinary teenage world, and talent cut him off still more. In a few short years a teenage boy finds himself the size of a man, but unable to impose order upon his world as a man can. There are the doubts, the fears of failure, the self-consciousness. All the different elements of life whirl around in his head. If he asks a girl for a date, will she say no? If he asks a girl for a date, will she say yes, and if she does what then? The word *yes* opens up a whole range of possibilities, and like anything unknown it is viewed with a mixture of curiosity and fear. Stevie had all the usual mixed-up feelings of the average teenager, and then some. Would his blindness turn girls off? He refused to go on a date with a chaperone, but at the same time he was embarrassed to ask some girl, probably as nervous as he was, to describe the movie, help him out of the cab, tell him what was going on, read the menu to him in a restaurant. Perhaps there was the illogical feeling that the girl would start back in dismay, and say, "Why didn't you tell me you were blind?" Growing up hurts a good deal.

It wasn't that girls ignored him. They mobbed his concerts, screaming for Stevie, trying to touch Stevie, trying to get Stevie's autograph. But there is privacy in a crowd, and no privacy at all, no protection from just one other human being.

And aside from all those problems there was Motown, a kind of stern corporate father, sitting up with an eye on the living room clock waiting for him to show up when he said he would. Ready to lecture him if he was ten minutes late. His allowance had grown from the original $2.50 a week, but Stevie was impatient to get on with adult life, to be free of constraint.

There was the pressure of performance, the soaring high and the rapid coming down to earth afterward. There was the money. Stevie knew he would be a millionaire when his trust fund was released to him when he was twenty-one. But it seemed as though he'd been working his entire life. For a poor black kid from the Detroit ghetto, it was a strange world, a world in bits and pieces. Home was at the other end of a telephone most of the time, and the rest of life was work, study, performance. Anxious to take good care of him, his corporate parent had raised him very strictly as to personal habits. No swearing, no smoking, and certainly no drugs or drinking. Enough sleep each night, homework assignments must be done on time. Corporations are not known for their sense of responsibility, much less for a sense of decency, but Motown took care of Stevie Wonder, and it wasn't the mere protection of an investment. They really did have the best of intentions toward Stevie Wonder, human being. They may have seemed puritanical and restrictive from Stevie's point of view, but it was the kind of puritanism and restrictiveness that millions of American kids could have done with. It expressed a very caring attitude toward the young star.

He might feel constricted by the structured life he led, but it did protect him from the outside world, from being alone, from racism,

Stevie was one of the performers at the kick-off night of a "Summer in the Park" in June 1969. The crowd assembled at the Washington Monument grounds had been restless and some of them had booed Mrs. Richard Nixon, who presided over the ceremonies. Stevie helped calm the crowd, and Mrs. Nixon later expressed her appreciation. With them is Mayor Walter Washington of Washington, D.C. *(United Press International)*

from numerous unknown things. He had left his own home at a very young age, and the people at Motown had been fathers, mothers, uncles, brothers, friends to him. Cutting loose would be a painful necessity, very painful.

He had the extreme fluctuations of mood that all teenagers suffer, and he had them worse because he was an artist, a performer. There was his blindness. A disability must be adjusted to all one's life. But the very word "adjust" made it sound simpler than it was, a mere tightening of some essential nut. He thought of drugs to kill the pain of existence, but Motown helped him through the difficult months, persuading him that drugs would destroy him as a musician . They were older than he was, they knew that the teenage horrors do pass with time, that life becomes more stable, becomes manageable. And Stevie hung on, and came through. He has said, "If I were high it would destroy the character of my music, because I would be tripping out so much on myself as opposed to the things around me or what I was seeing, as opposed to the conclusions I've come to within my own mind."

He says, "I never did acid or anything like that, but I did try grass a couple of times. The first time was pretty nice, I got out there, but the next time was nothing but a lot of paranoia so I never went near it again. I love to hear people talking about all the junk I must be doing, though. You know, 'There goes Stevie Wonder jiving around. Must be stoned again.' Sometimes I'll be sitting somewhere listening to tapes, like on a plane or something, and my head'll get to going around like it does when I hear music, and I'll hear somebody whisper, 'Look at Stevie Wonder over there actin' crazy. You reckon he on dope?' That's so funny. First of all, they figure that 'cause you're blind you can't hear them. And my moving my head around like that, that's just what is called a blindism."

Although by his mid-teens he had learned to control his blindisms except when he was playing, they did prevent him from getting offers to appear on television in America. TV producers thought that Stevie's blindisms would not go down well with audiences, would "make the audience nervous." It was exposure that he needed very badly during those teenage years, but he didn't get it. Perhaps the TV executives felt nervous themselves when they watched him, not understanding that the head movements were Stevie's way of getting rid of the excess energy which sighted people get rid of by looking and seeing. They acknowledged his success in clubs like Marty's on Hill and even at New York's Philharmonic Hall, where he appeared in October 1969, but did not feel it would "go" on television. He appeared on European television during those years, very successfully, but the less plastic approach to the media in Europe meant that they were looking for performers who came across as "real," and audiences loved him, blindisms and all.

Stevie, and Motown, were approaching the crisis point. The corporation itself, or more accurately its "sound," was going through an identity crisis, engendered by changes in musical tastes and the introduction, primarily through the influence of the San Francisco group Sly and the Family Stone, of a more acid, funky type of rock which some had dubbed "funkedelic" or "acid soul." Motown's reaction had been to dip a toe into the boiling waters and snatch it back. The Temptations' "Cloud Nine" can best be described as Stevie described it: "a combination of rhythm and blues, psychedelic and a funky African-type beat." Simultaneously, Motown went even more conservative, not just sticking to the gradually evolving "Motown sound" but actually re-releasing old hits, among others, Martha and the Vandellas' "Dancing in the Streets." Never mind that the record made the charts, such a move, in Stevie's opinion, just wasn't progressive.

"I'm experimenting," he announced. "A lot of things I've done recently are funkedelic." To look at him, one would not expect it. There he was, nineteen years old, and still wearing his hair close-cropped, dressed in the same suits he wore at the age of fifteen, just a few sizes larger. In appearance, he was simply a taller version of Little Stevie Wonder. And his records, though always carrying his personal stamp, still basically embodied the Motown

Arrangements made between Motown and the Michigan School for the Blind enabled Stevie to be on the road performing during much of the school year. He graduated in June 1969 at the age of nineteen, and with his diploma and a congratulatory kiss from his mother, he also received a special citation for his "awe-inspiring life" from the Michigan Legislature. *(United Press International)*

sound.

Not that it was unsuccessful. "Yester-Me, Yester-You, Yesterday," released in October 1969, not only became a gold record in the United States, it was the first of his records to reach the Number One spot on the British charts. Though Stevie was of course pleased with the success of the record, he felt he had gone beyond it. "It should have been a hit in 1967," he explained. "We recorded it two years ago as an album track, it should have been on the album after 'Down to Earth.' But somehow it got left off. I recorded it at the same time as 'My Cherie Amour.' " It was not Stevie Wonder, 1969. In fact, there were times when Stevie wondered who Stevie Wonder was, anyhow.

Back in 1968, he had recorded an album called "Eivets Rednow." "It was a completely different thing for me," explains Stevie. "I had written some things on it for the late Wes Montgomery, but he died before he could record them." So Stevie had decided to record them himself, along with "Alfie" and other instrumentals. He had also decided not to issue it under his own name. "Eivets Rednow" is "Stevie Wonder" spelled backwards. "Some people [knew], some didn't," says Stevie. "As a matter of fact there was a cat in the airport that came up and said, 'Hey, man,' he said. 'Man, those whites takin' over everything.... Look, I heard a kid today, man, played "Alfie" just *like* you man!' 'Oh yeah, this cat named Rednow?' 'Yeah, that's it!' I said, 'Ooooh, man, that cat is—well, don't worry about *him*!' " Needless to say, the people at Motown pulled some long faces over that one. "I must say Motown did not push it," says Stevie. They were pulling long faces a lot those days. Stevie grew a moustache. Motown, in the person of Stevie's musical director, Gene Kee, started saying he had the potential to be another Sammy Davis. "By the time he's twenty-one he will have become Stevie Wonder, the Entertainer, and not just Stevie Wonder, the maker of pop records," said Kee in April 1969.

Stevie was not so sure. Although he still enjoyed performing, he was re-thinking his relationship to the music world. "I've been doing a lot of writing lately and some producing over the last two months," he told a reporter in December of 1969. "I've produced sessions with Martha and the Vandellas, Rita Wright and some of the new groups on the new underground label Rare Earth. I've been doing some underground things myself.... I'd like to do a lot

In February 1970, while on a trip to New York, Stevie visited the Eye Institute of the Columbia Presbyterian Medical Center and presented copies of his record albums to the young patients. He was the recipient of the Fight for Sight Show Business Inspiration Award of 1969 for his "compelling achievements in the world of entertainment." *(Wide World Photos)*

more producing. Eventually I want to just write and produce . . ." These activities seemed more solid, more substantial than merely performing, and the temporariness of things occupied his mind a lot at that period.

Benny Benjamin, Motown's first studio drummer, died that year, and Stevie had foreseen his death. The drummer had been hospitalized following a stroke. Everyone, including Stevie, had been sure he would recover. Then Stevie had a dream. He was talking with Benny, telling him not to worry, that everything would be all right. But Benny was terribly weak, and he told Stevie he was

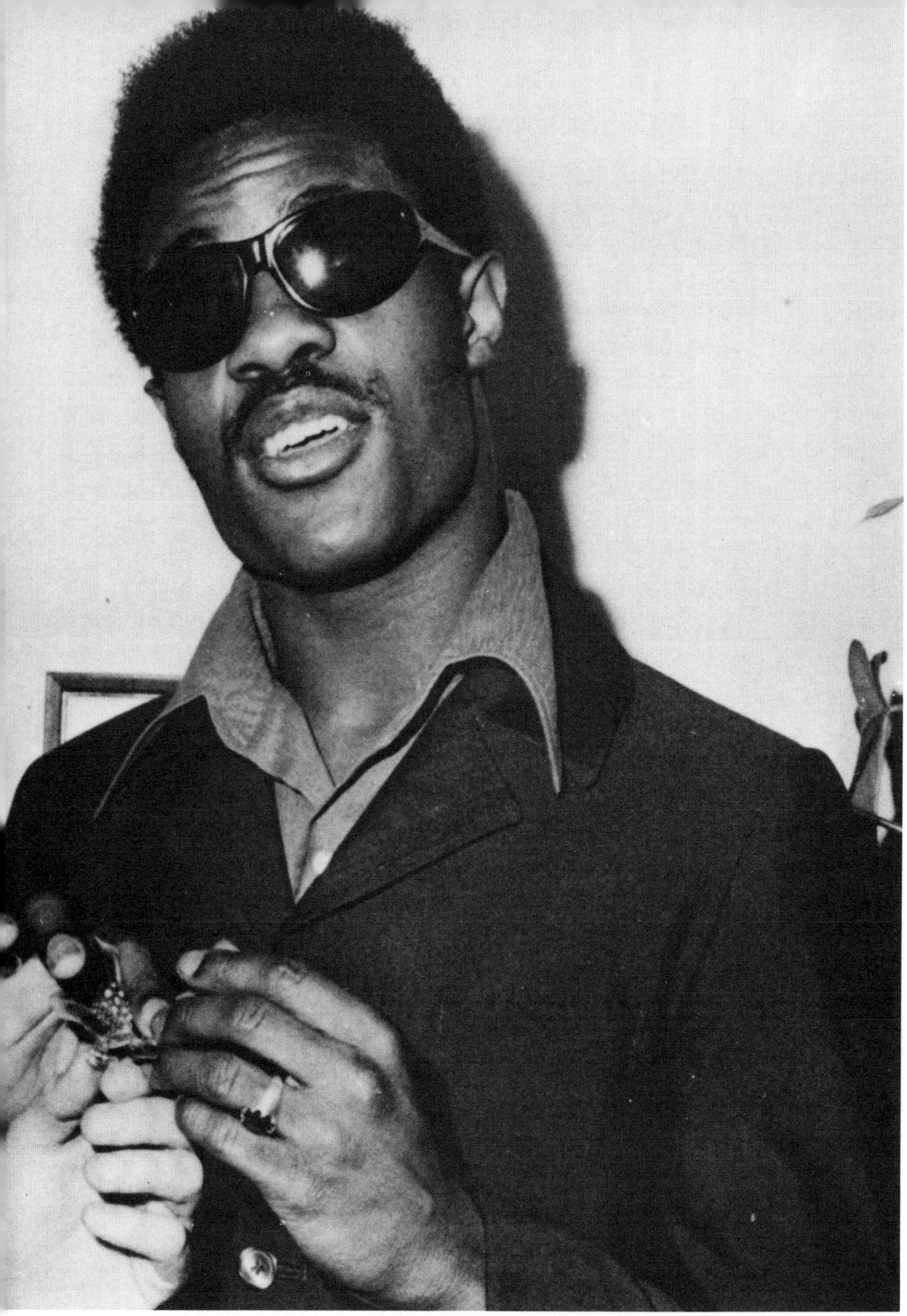

While in New York to play a two-week engagement at the Copacabana in March 1970, Stevie attended a performance of the play, "Butterflies Are Free." Afterward, he went backstage to visit Keir Dullea, who played the young blind musician in the show. *(Wide World Photos)*

wrong; he was sure he was going to die. The dream occurred on a Wednesday. The following Sunday, Benny Benjamin was dead. What had Benny left behind, Stevie asked himself, but the echoes of his drum beats in a few people's minds. "I would like to write more and stop singing so much," Stevie announced. "I like writing even more than singing. With writing you leave something behind."

Stevie had always paid attention to his dreams. They were so vivid that they had the quality of real life. He has said that dreams are his life, and during that period, when he was struggling with the problems of who he was, in relationship to Motown, in relationship to the rest of the world and to himself, he became more and more introspective, seeking in his dreams—so filled with sound and smell and touch—and in his waking fantasies, escape from the difficult realities of blindness and dependence and youth. He escaped into his dreams, and into his music.

For some years, the wide spectrum of songs in each of his albums had indicated his straining at the Motown bounds. *Up Tight* had featured "Blowin' in the Wind;" *Down to Earth* had included "Mr. Tambourine Man" as well as a song popularized by the Supremes, "My World Is Empty Without You;" and his first *Greatest Hits* collection had included "Castles in the Sand" and "Hey Harmonica Man." Interspersed with the standard Motown fluff were songs popularized by other artists, selections in which he took instrumental license. More and more his personal stamp was evident as he wrote and recorded his own songs and won the right to record those of others, and as he became more interested in writing and producing it was natural that he should want to produce one of his own albums. His opportunity came when the single "Signed, Sealed and Delivered," released in June 1970, reached number three in the charts and stayed there for fourteen weeks. The success of the single naturally called for an album of that title, and Stevie produced it entirely himself.

In doing so, he entered the realm of the musical expert, as well as taking on the awesome responsibility of "making" the album. In the electronic, mechanized, multichannel, synthesized world of modern recording, the performer is secondary. The sounds he produces are merely the raw material which the producer then molds and shapes with the help of artificial sounds, overlays of sound upon sound, electronically introduced reverberation, directional interplay and a plethora of other devices wholly beyond the ken of the layman. But Stevie Wonder was equal to the task. "He has an extremely analytical mind—particularly for music," Gene Kee once said. "When he heard Roland Kirk [the late blind jazz saxophonist] at Ronnie Scott's he was aware that Roland uses that circular breathing technique after four bars. And that's a very subtle thing." As a New York *Post* critic said, Stevie has flawless taste, and a perfect ear, and if the raw material with which he was working was his own he had no hangups about it. For Stevie, who recognizes no night and day, the production of *Signed, Sealed and*

Delivered involved round-the-clock sessions in the Motown recording studios, but he reveled in this first opportunity to exercise such considerable artistic control. He had the time of his life, and his efforts bore fruit. The album *Signed, Sealed and Delivered* won an award for the best soul album of 1970.

Although the award pleased him, Stevie was disappointed at this categorization. "People ask me what soul is," he had said a couple of years earlier, "but all people have soul. Soul is what you feel and you have what you feel. So anybody can have soul and you can call it what you want." The label-appliers in the music business would have their way, however, and Stevie Wonder still labors under that artificial categorization.

But recognition is recognition. Stevie Wonder was emerging from the teenage pop R&B world and gaining respect among important music critics. Beginning in 1969, he played well-known clubs like the Cellar Door in Washington, D.C., and the Village Gate in New York City. And in March of 1970 he appeared at the famed Copacabana. The event signaled a landmark of sorts in his career. First, it was one of the most successful shows the Copa had enjoyed in years. His ninety-minute performance was just not enough for the SRO audience, who demanded a seemingly endless series of encores and, as one critic put it, "Yelled themselves hoarse for 'more.' " Anyone who got that kind of recognition at the Copa made the music world snap to attention. More important was the new respect on the part of the critics. One at the New York *Post* wrote of him: " . . . an honest prodigy of flawless taste and superb talent. Not only has he developed his own style as a soul singer, but he's one of the world's virtuosos on the chromatic harmonica."

And a writer for the *Village Voice,* reviewing Stevie's performance at the Apollo, where he played a week in August 1970, was particularly impressed by Stevie's effort on the next to last day of his stand, by the way he performed "as if his real contract is not with the management but with the people out front."

The critic continued: "The blind led the sighted into inner space. I was not prepared for it. Stevie Wonder had come to mean 'Cherie Amour' and some of the pat AM hits accompanied by violins. Heard last Monday at the seven o'clock show he was to be trusted, delighted to be sharing his music with whoever was out there, and natural as a willow tree. He was also in rough voice, straining for his mid-high range, but needing those notes badly enough to go after them until he had had his say. . . .I don't know what he had left for the evening show, but I suspect that it was something beautiful, something new, and something an audience member might feel happy to take home with him."

Stevie Wonder was doing what is so difficult for a child star. He was making the transition to adulthood without losing his popularity, gaining the respect of the critics with his own unique talent, for which he was beholden to nobody. Motown deserved a lot of credit, but more and more the credit was all Stevie's. He was growing up. Then again, so was Motown.

"You see, Motown is like big enough to called an organization, but it's also small enough to be called a family," Stevie had said back in 1967. But things at Motown were changing. The company had grown as it had prospered, and by 1970, following the general westward trend of the technological entertainment industry, Gordy had begun to move some of his operations out to Los Angeles, establishing two branches of the firm with all the increased complexity that involved. "The things is Tamla used to be just a company, but now it's a corporation, so there are more people involved, one has less time to be friends with everyone," Stevie explained in the summer of 1970. "Also, a lot of people have moved to the West Coast, for instance. So of course a lot of the family atmosphere has gone. This I think happens in any business when it grows.from a company to a corporation. I expect when Henry Ford started making cars he sat around and grooved and chatted, but then more became involved and the atmosphere was lost. And in a business like the recording industry you can't always have a family relationship with everyone, although you would love to. You have people involved who are just interested in doing their job, making their money and getting home." In a way, it was unfortunate that Motown was becoming big and impersonal. But it would make it easier for Stevie when it came time to make the break.

For some years, Stevie had had things to say musically that did not fit into the Motown mold. By 1970 he also had a life to lead which was his own and not the corporation's. He had an independence of mobility that some found amazing in a blind person. Arriving in London during a tour in the summer of 1970, he was helped out of a limousine in front of the Talk of the Town, then surprised reporters by finding the door himself, opening it and walking down a short passage, up a flight of stairs and into his dressing room, completely unaided. He also had an emotional life of his own. He had fallen in love with Syreeta Wright, sister to Motown singer Rita Wright. A former secretary at Motown, Syreeta had musical aspirations of her own, and she and Stevie had fallen in love to background music of their own. She accompanied him to Britain on that tour, and they chose to announce their engagement in London on June 18, 1970.

But all these were pretty much natural concomitants to growing up. His independence from Motown was somewhat different. Typically enough, Stevie's statement of discontent with Motown was expressed in music. He had a new album in the works, one that he promised would boast a new style of songwriting. "A lot of the things on my new album deal with the social problems, it's completely different, it's more me than anything I have done before," he had said earlier that year. "I have been influenced by the things that have happened in the world. I've been writing like this for a long time, but this is the first time [the people at] Motown have given me the chance to do it . . . this album will express my true thoughts, it's not Motown, it's me, and Syreeta Wright, my fiancée, who helped me with the lyrics . . . . Unfortunately, artists get put in a bag, which I disagree with, but with this LP I will get the chance to do different things."

Released later in 1970 and aptly titled, considering Stevie's hopes for it, *Where I'm Coming From* was the work of a mature Stevie, on his way out of the Motown formula into a style entirely his own. Although some critics thought *Where I'm Coming From* was an uneasy compromise, partly Stevie but partly Motown, lyrically unremarkable and at times seeming to reach too far for uniqueness and contemporariness, it served its purpose in Stevie's development. An artist must take one step at a time, and the work that is done each year is related to the work of the previous years. Only the individual artist can judge how fast he should progress from step to step.

But listen to "*Fingertips*" and then listen to "*Where I'm Coming From*" and you can tell what those ten years meant in the development of Stevie Wonder. Whatever the imperfections of

Stevie and Syreeta Wright announced their engagement in London on June 30, 1970. Syreeta was hoping for a singing career, and the two looked forward to a life of musical collaboration. *(United Press International)*

Right: **Stevie and Syreeta were married in Detroit in the summer of 1970. Motown hosted the reception for its star and its former secretary.** *(United Press International)*

Where I'm Coming From, the child prodigy had indeed become a man. It was no small triumph. One of the hardest things that the child prodigy has to suffer through is that time when he discovers all of a sudden that it doesn't "come naturally." The crisis often occurs in the teens when the pressures of the world build up. What has seemed like a "natural ability," as easy as walking or climbing a tree, is suddenly understood to be incredibly complex. Stevie weathered that storm, and came out the other side a mature artist. And into his music would come the feeling of the times. As a kid, he remembered, "The history of this country was relatively boring—I guess because of the way it was put to us in books. The most interesting to me was about civilizations before ours, how advanced people really were, how high they had brought themselves only to bring themselves down because of the missing links, the weak foundations. So the whole thing crumbled. And that's kind of sad. And it relates to today and what could possibly happen here, very soon." No subsequent album would be without at least one "political" song.

"I speak of the history, the heritage of the violence, or the negativeness of being able to see what's going on with minority people. Seemingly it's going to continue to be this way. Sometimes unfortunately violence is a way things get accomplished. 'Big Brother' was something to make people aware of the fact that after all is said and done, that I don't have to do nothing to you, meaning the people are now power players. We don't have to do anything to them 'cause they're gonna cause their own country to fall."

When the time came for Stevie's contract to be renewed again, he was twenty-one years old and more than ready and able to leave his Motown home and strike out on his own. He played for time, stalled six months, hired an outside auditor to go over the Motown accounts. Motown is notoriously secretive about the actual numbers of records sold, refusing to submit to a public audit in order to have its gold records certified by the Recording Industry Association of America. Reassured that all was well, Stevie asked for his contract back. Ewert Abner, president of Motown, reports that "He came to see me and said, 'I'm twenty-one now. I'm not gonna do what you say anymore. Void my contract.' I freaked."

"They were upset at first," Stevie recalls. "But they began to understand—later. Whatever peak I had reached doing that kind of music, I had reached. It was important for them to understand we were going nowhere. I wasn't growing. I just kept repeating the Stevie Wonder sound, and it didn't express how I felt about what was happening out there. I decided to go for something besides a winning formula. I wanted to see what would happen if I changed. It challenged me to give the public something other than what it was used to hearing."

Stevie performed at the Apollo Theater in Harlem many times while he was with Motown, and Apollo audiences watched him develop from a child star to an adult performer. Merely one act in the Motown Revue when he was a child, by 1970 he was presenting full concerts with his own band and singing group, "Wonderlove." *(Wide World Photos)*

Stevie was not short of advice. People were only too willing to tell him about the headaches involved in striking out on his own. He would have to make distribution deals, start his own companies for recording, hire the right lawyers. The music world is a high-powered, fast-moving business. He would have to be more than a star performer to survive; he would have to be a star at business, too. Being blind, he would be open to exploitation. But Stevie was determined to take the plunge anyway. He was twenty-one. It was time to be on his own. It was just *time*.

5

Out on His Own

(Sue Cassidy Clark)

Stevie was not the first artist to leave Motown on reaching age twenty-one, but he would be one of the few from the early Motown roster who would do so successfully. Mary Wells and Kim Weston had tried it, and had not been heard from again. Talent alone was not enough for the independent artist. An organization was necessary, trustworthy aides, a good lawyer, people with loyalty and good business sense.

One of the first people Stevie hired after he left Motown was Ira Tucker, who began as his publicist, later served as his road manager, and now functions as a sort of combination confidant/aide-de-camp. The two had met through Motown; Ira's sister, Linda Lawrence, had been one of the Supremes. Tucker, a former schoolteacher with considerable songwriting talent and an excellent singing voice, is very protective of Stevie, and the two enjoy a close relationship. Stevie's older brother, Calvin, also joined his organization. Another fortunate choice was Johanan Vigoda as Stevie's attorney. The three men provided a solid and reliable base of support in the everchanging, fast-moving world of

(Peter Gould/Keystone)

Out on his own and answerable to no one but himself, Stevie experienced a creative spurt. Melodies, lyrics, riffs came to him constantly, and even when he was eating he made sure his tape recorder was within easy reach. *(Pictorial Parade)*

Stevie wowed them in Brazil, where he toured in 1971, although his music did not at that time contain Brazilian rhythms. He would later incorporate Brazilian rhythms and lyrics into his music, and his trip to Brazil was undoubtedly a major influence in his later musical development. *(Pictorial Parade)*

the music business.

Stevie wanted complete independence, and total control over every phase of his music. He and his small organization packed up and moved to New York where his own production company, Taurus Productions, and his own publishing company, Black Bull Music, Inc., would be established and where Stevie rented studio space at Electric Lady Studios, gathered around him every musical instrument he could think of, and started making music. He and Syreeta began work on a new album to mark Stevie's coming of age.

The album was not intended to hit the charts, for it was to be such a radical departure from the Motown Stevie Wonder sound that Stevie fully expected it would not be understood by some of his record-buying fans. Not only was it to be new in lyrical and rhythmic concept, it would be new in terms of production, for on it Stevie would employ for the first time electronic sound synthesizers.

First developed in 1955 and continually being refined since then, the music synthesizer is a computerized instrument that can be programmed to produce musical effects far beyond the range and versatility of conventional musical instruments.

"With it," says Stevie, "you have the ability to shape the melody into any form you desire: attack, sustain, delay, release or the combination of those can be done any way you want to create the sound. You can only play one note at a time, though, with the synthesizer, so I use the Moog for certain horn lines, but it really is not so much to imitate as to make the horizon for an instrument even wider. I also use the ARP synthesizer, which I program myself and have become very attached to."

Two highly talented musicians programmed the Moog synthesizer. Robert Margouleff and Malcolm Cecil of Tonto's Expanding Head Band had produced a record that made heavy use of the synthesizer, a record called "Tonto's Expanding Head." Stevie met them through Ritchie Havens. "He was doing a session one night with them and I'd been listening to Walter Carlos's *Switched-On Bach* and thought I'd like to do some things with [the synthesizer]." Few other black musicians were using the synthesizer, even in experimental form, and most white musicians who used it did so with an ear toward gimmickry. But Stevie saw greater potential in the technological advance. The synthesizer

Stevie considers himself lucky to live in the era of the computer. The music synthesizer has made possible an artistic control earlier musicians could only dream about. Other uses of the synthesizer are being developed to help the blind. Here, Dr. John Eulenberg, inventor of a computer synthesizer that "reads" Braille vocally, shows Stevie how the instrument operates. (Kwame Brathwaite)

made possible even more artistic control for Stevie. Not only could he do all parts of a number himself, he could control every aspect of the sound, the balance, the total effect. The experience of creating in the New York studio, with its wonderland of electronic equipment, was comparable to that when he was a little nine-year-old blind boy from the Detroit ghetto suddently let loose in the Hitsville recording studios.

Stevie is a high-energy person who can go all night and all day, working around the clock in the studio to get something exactly the way he wants it to be. He is a hard-driving perfectionist to the point of tedium. And yet behind the devastating work schedules that wear out lesser men lies the fact that Stevie as an adult has retained the marvelous gift of being able to play with sound with the same kind of enthusiasm and lightness of touch that he had as a child. It is this ability to "play," to express pure human delight through sound, that sets the adult genius of music apart from the mere practitioner. There is a level at which the mature artist must remain "free" in spirit, able to dance and turn cartwheels musically, when they are necessary artistically. There is an effortlessness and seeming simplicity in the most complex works of a true artist. Stevie's new album, *Music of My Mind,* would show a man at work, a man with a technical ability so well assimilated that it did not intrude upon the spirit of the music, but supported it lightly.

In *Music of My Mind* he played piano, drums, harmonica, organ, clavichord, clavinet (electric piano) and synthesizers, and he sang most of the background vocals. He had been studying electronic equipment since his middle teens, and this technical background was invaluable in helping him get the effect he wanted. Rather than being at the mercy of someone else's technical knowledge, he mastered the machines just as he had the harmonica and the drums so many years earlier. The electronic equipment became an extension of Stevie's magic world, expressing what he wanted to say.

The album was some months in production, and though he worked on it steadily he took time to perform as well. No longer booked for concerts and other guest appearances by Motown, he had to establish contacts and keep his name alive as a performer in order to ensure maximum exposure for his post-Motown records. He hired a seven-piece band, which he named Wonderlove, three female singers (the lead singer was Linda, Ira Tucker's sister), and with his entourage toured the East Coast under the title "The Stevie Wonder Review." In September, while performing in Atlantic City, New Jersey, Stevie received word that he had been elected to ASCAP as a songwriter member. The American Society of Composers and Performers the premier organization in the music world. Election to membership was for Stevie not only an honor but a gratifying recognition of his newly achieved independence.

Over the next few months the band was expanded to twelve pieces, including several soloists, and the Stevie Wonder Review members meshed and developed an excellent show that further demonstrated both the star's versatility and his ever-increasing musical distance from Motown. The obligatory performances of some of his fairly recent hits notwithstanding, the clearly defined direction was toward jazz improvisation, and while continuing to play at rock concerts (the group did a series of rock performances in Britain in January-February 1972, Stevie's tenth tour there), in March and April of 1972 the group was booked into one of New York City's foremost jazz spots, The Bitter End. "He and his band had that joint rocking like I've never heard it rock," wrote Carman Moore of the *Village Voice* some months later. "Stevie knows it—he lit up when I mentioned it and called it the greatest thing he's ever done."

Other critics disagreed, however. One wrote of his Bitter End performance, "Every time he got into interesting and progressive music, his Motown background pulled him back." Others persisted in overlooking or deliberately ignoring his developing jazz idiom and continued to call him a soul artist.

One of Stevie's justifiable complaints has always been that people who *write* about music are always categorizing the people who *make* music. "People are always labeling you . . . as a performer . . . rather than listening to whatever it is you're doing and accepting you for what you are. I mean, they're always trying to *comprehend* you, you see, and they think that by saying, hey, I got that cat's *label*—you understand?—that they have you all figured out. You can say . . . well *this* dude here is obviously a rock singer . . . or this cat here has a country-western thing . . . . So now that I know what he *is*, I know *all about him*! Well, you don't know *shit*!

Stevie complained that there were even people who had been heard to remark that his music "didn't sound like Stevie Wonder." "How can I not sound like *me*? That's not my problem, when that happens. That's the problem of somebody who has . . . jumped to conclusions too quickly."

Recognizing that it is hard enough to do what you really want to do, to be truly free artistically, Stevie does not see why he should be boxed in. When he wants to do a show consisting of old songs, whether it is "Fingtertips" and his other hits from the past, or other people's songs, he does it. And because he is doing what he feels like doing that night, and he is singing what he feels like singing, the audience feels good with him, and the show is a success. But

On his own now, Stevie demonstrated his independence from Motown by wearing African-style clothing and his hair in "corn rows." But his most important departure from the Motown formula was his use of the musical synthesizer. (Peter Gould/*Keystone)*

***Overleaf:* By the summer of 1973, barely two-and-a-half years since he had left Motown, Stevie had produced three one-man albums. He worked like a man obsessed, putting his musical ideas into tangible form, working against the clock inside his head that seemed to be ticking off the moments to that "something" he felt was going to happen.** *(Wide World Photos)*

THESIZER

(Sue Cassidy Clark)

When it was announced that Stevie would tour with the Rolling Stones as their opening, or warm-up, act in the summer of 1972, many people were surprised. But Stevie was willing to play "second fiddle" in exchange for the exposure he knew the Stones tour would bring him. *(Wide World Photos)*

though the audience may be happy, the critics may pull long faces, complaining that he is repeating himself. It is almost as though they are afraid to listen to the same song twice.

"Now, *I* was enjoying myself," he would complain, "and the audiences, they were enjoying themselves . . . and yet people seemed to take this as a sign that I was never going to do anything worthwhile again. Which is stupid, naturally."

By early 1972, Stevie had laid down forty-four musical tracks on which he played all the instruments. The bulk of the material went into *Music of My Mind.* Yet the album was only on tapes. Mass album production requires an organization and physical facilities far larger than Stevie's infant enterprise could handle. The same was true of distribution. Stevie needed an established company to mass-produce and distribute the album properly, a company like Motown. But he did not have to go begging to Gordy's company; Motown came to him. People at Motown had kept an eye on their former star and big money-maker and had heard the excited talk about Stevie's new album that ran through music circles. Stevie Wonder must be wooed back, it was decided, on any terms.

With attorney Johanan Vigoda, Stevie negotiated a new contract with Motown. The terms included more money—a lot more money—and Stevie's right to considerable artistic control over his music, production of his records and bookings for his personal appearances. In effect, Motown would act as distributors of his records and handle advertising, and Stevie would have the freedom and the resources to create as he wanted to, without interference, with few strings attached.

Only one other artist, Marvin Gaye, had managed to get Motown to accede to that kind of independence. Other artists had been forced to leave the "Motown family" and sign with other labels—the Spinners, the Four Tops, Martha Reeves of Martha and the Vandellas were some. "I think if they feel they have to go somewhere else to get what they need they should do it," Stevie has said. "I feel that Motown did a lot of good things for the artists, but some bad things did happen. I think what happened with a lot of artists—even the Supremes—was that you had the writers, Holland-Dozier-Holland. After they came up with the basic formula they just cut tracks and tracks and tracks. They would just cut tracks even before they knew the key or if the artists would be suitable singers for the song." Stevie's new contract ensured

Bob McAllister of "Wonderama" interviews Stevie, who is a favorite with the show's young audience.
(Kwame Brathwaite)

that he would be bound by no such restricting formula, but it had been necessary for him to leave Motown in order to get it. He was satisfied to continue his relationship with Motown on his own terms. "I basically feel that I'm not really into business, though I do know how I would like certain things to be run." He started running things early. People at Motown suggested some changes in *Music of My Mind,* but Stevie, who had the album virtually finished by the time the new contract was signed, did not take a single one of the suggestions. "He had enough insight to see what he needed to sustain Stevie Wonder as an individual, not just as a product of a record company," explains Ira Tucker. "It's kind of awesome. I tend to think he had it all figured out from the time he was fourteen. Basically, God manages Stevie, and Stevie manages himself."

Released in early May on the Motown/Tamla label, *Music of My Mind* received almost universal critical acclaim. The New York *Times* critic Don Neckman said, "One-man recordings have been tried by other performers . . . but no one has brought off the complicated trick of playing most—or all—of the parts better than Wonder in this collection. After a few minutes of the first track, one promptly forgets all about the technical legerdemain and settles down to hear a constantly provocative flow of musical ideas, good humor, artistic invention and solid swing."

In Britain, people were calling *Music of My Mind* Stevie Wonder's *Sgt. Pepper*, referring to the album considered the Beatles' most successful. "I'm not sure that labels like that really help, but I know what they mean," one British critic wrote. "Like *Pepper*, there is a wholeness about this album which is completely satisfying: each track is a real song, beautifully constructed, instantly memorable and self-contained. Yet the tracks hang together and complement each other perfectly . . . [and] it is the first completely successful integration of the Moog in a pop context. Suffice it to say that it's the first time I've ever thought of it as a musical instrument rather than a gadget."

(Kwame Brathwaite)

The Beatles were four; Stevie is one. Apart from brief instrumental solos by guitarist Buzzy Feton on "Superwoman" and trombonist Art Baron on "Love Having You Around," Stevie had played every single note on the album. And although Syreeta and her sister, Yvonne Wright, had collaborated on some of the lyrics, most of these were Stevie's as well. Lyrically, *Music of My Mind* was far superior to *Where I'm Coming From*, much more sharply focused and far less preachy. Critical praise for his lyrics was a particularly new and pleasing experience for Stevie.

Although he was gratified by the critical acclaim, Stevie was anxious to take his music to the audience in the form of live performance, and because *Music of My Mind* was a statement of the new Stevie Wonder, who had broken out of the confines of soul, he felt he wanted to take his music to a new audience. For most of his career, Stevie's audience had been black. Motown was a black-owned label and had always concentrated on the black market. Although increasingly the influence of black music could be heard in the music of white performers, some of whom freely acknowledged that influence, there remained a separation between the races in the music world: white generally bought

white and black bought black. Stevie thought this a needless and counterproductive separation. "If you think of blacks and whites in separate terms, you're feeding off of something that's dying every day," he says, "You're feeding off of something that I just never eat."

So Stevie decided to join the Rolling Stones for their national tour in the late spring and early summer of 1972. He would be their opening act, and he chose to do so over the objections of many of his advisors. They objected that the world would think Stevie Wonder, the star, who had toured with top billing with the Stones eight years earlier, was washed up if he had to be their opening act, that he obviously couldn't make it on his own. But Stevie believed the tour would be good for his career and that whatever his position in the show's billing it would give him the kind of national exposure to young white audiences that he felt he and *Music of My Mind* needed.

After sellout concerts in some fifty cities, the tour wound up with several SRO performances at New York's Madison Square Garden. It had been a sensational tour for the Stones and all in all a relatively satisfying one for Stevie, but there had been hassles. One night one of the key members of Stevie's band, his drummer, had refused to show and Stevie had been unable to make one of the performances. There had been times when he had played to audiences restless in anticipation of seeing the Stones and unwilling to listen to him, an insult every warmup act suffers at times. And certain promotional failures rankled with Stevie. "If I had it to do over again, I'd insist upon certain things being handled differently," he said. "For one thing, my name hasn't been on all the marquees where we played. I think it should have been . . . And there are other things: the amount of time I have to play, and the way the publicity is handled. But . . . I don't blame the Stones for these problems so much as the people who put the thing together, and even myself, for not making sure about the way the tour was arranged ahead of time." Fortunately, Stevie would never again have to be a warmup act.

The tour had accomplished what Stevie had wanted. "At least it lets people know I'm not doing 'Fingertips' anymore," he said wryly. Exposure had been the thing, and many people had been introduced to him and his music on the tour. "I like to have a lot of time to stretch out—to get that spirit moving—and we only got to

When Stevie left Motown, he knew he would not be successful unless he had people he could trust in his organization. Both of his older brothers, Calvin, shown here, and Milton, went to work for him. (Kwame Brathwaite)

HOHNER

Innervisions was important to Stevie, his most importance ablum to date, in his mind. Its release marked the first time Stevie held a press preview for one of his albums. Flanked by his brother, Milton Hardaway, he greeted the assembled reporters and photographers. (Sue Cassidy Clark)

Stevie explained that the assembled press people were to be taken on a bus trip and that they would be blindfolded so that they would hear the sounds of the city that he heard and that had prompted the album cut, "Living for the City." (Sue Cassidy Clark)

Left: Stevie is a marvel at nearly every instrument he attempts to play. (Kwame Brathwaite)

play for thirty or forty minutes, but we've still managed to make a lot of people have soulful experiences." Indeed, there had been many people turned on to his sound for the first time who had stood and cheered the end of his set. He'd not behaved like a warmup performer; he had *burned*, and few who had seen him could forget him. "Spectacular as the Stones were . . . ,"wrote a New York *Times* critic, "my most vivid musical memories are of the charged-up playing and singing of the blind soul singer/musician Stevie Wonder and his crisp little band, Wonderlove." By the time the tour ended, with Stevie joining Mick Jagger in a memorable rendition of "Satisfaction," Stevie's audience had tripled.

It could not have happened at a more auspicious time. It was a time when white rock groups and singers had come to rely on weirdness to attract audiences, and they and their music became so alienated that the already alienated audiences who were looking to music in desperation for something to hang onto, were getting bizarre sideshows. While the white rock music of the fifties and sixties owed a great deal to black music, it was white performers who had made the names and the money during those decades. The audiences did not give up on white rock singers—there was an eerie attractiveness about their bold anti-establishment antics—but they found in black music satisfying new expressions of feeling, with a classic quality that gave them longterm value rather than fad success.

"Music can measure how broad our horizons are," said Stevie. "My mind wants to see infinity. 'Stevie Wonder is a camouflage. Through my music, I, Steveland Judkins Morris, my real name, have been able to express my deepest feelings and those of other people." This statement was a world away from boa constrictors and freaky eyeshadow, what had become the carnival atmosphere of white rock. And those audiences who were introduced to Stevie Wonder heard music about something real, music that was a solid expression about enduring in hard times, about love found and love lost, about poverty, about spirituality, and it helped an alienated generation begin to find a place to put their heads.

The national audience was ready for Stevie Wonder, and within a few months he provided a hit for them to buy. "Superstition," released in November 1972, hit Number One on the singles charts (his second Number One single after nearly a decade) and remained there sixteen weeks. Stevie had expected it to do well. He'd introduced "Superstition" on the tour with the Stones, and audiences had loved it. Lyrically, it was not particularly memorable; rhythmically, it was unforgettable. In recording it, Stevie had wired the ARP synthesizer to the clavinet, or electric piano, to produce an incessant, driving, wop-wop sound that defied the listener to keep still. It would be a sound often imitated by others and used again and again by Stevie himself on many of his most successful "funky" tunes.

Unfortunately, the song was a bone of contention among Stevie, one of his guitarists, Jeff Beck, and Motown. Stevie had written and done a track for "Superstition" with no clear idea of how he was going to use it. At about the same time he had written a tune called "Thelonius" for Beck, but Beck had not used it; he liked "Superstition." Stevie had offered to write a new song for Beck, but Beck had taken "Superstition." Then Motown had said it wanted Stevie's rendition issued as a single. Beck had already done two takes of "Superstition," on one of which Stevie had been on clavinet. Stevie had tried to stop Motown from issuing his version, but the company was so sure it would be a hit they would not cease production. So much for Stevie's complete independence; when contract time came, he decided, he would insist on the right to choose which songs would be released as singles. But Motown had been right about the success of the record. "Superstition" would help Stevie's next album, *Talking Book*, become the first of his platinum (over one million copies sold) albums.

Much of the material for *Talking Book* had been recorded at the same time as that for *Music of My Mind*, and indeed the two albums can be considered a hyphenated, dual statement, the first displaying his talent for total composition and production, the second applying these talents to the basic themes that had characterized his music and would continue to do so. Nearly all the cuts on *Talking Book* are about love—happy songs in a light, balladlike style and unhappy ones in the syncopated, funk style of "Superstition." But there is one political song, "Big Brother," and it foreshadowed similar interest in political tunes and the treatment of a variety of themes in one album.

Talking Book was acclaimed not just by record-buyers but by critics as well. Indeed, some still consider it his most perfect album.

"Every cut is a colorfully multi-tracked sonic canvas making heavy use of the synthesizer," said Stephen Holder in *Saturday Review*. He concluded his review by saying that it was "the most mature though not the most accessible album to date by a prodigious figure in pop music."

In many ways it was a very personal album, one in which Stevie revealed the results of his explorations into his own inner space. One has the feeling at times that there is much going on beneath the surface—of both the music and the lyrics—that one does not completely grasp. And yet there is much that is universally understandable and acceptable in the album. Besides "Superstition," "You Are the Sunshine of My Life" became a gold single and has been recorded vocally and instrumentally by many other artists. Frank Sinatra sang it in concert at Madison Square Garden. "Sunshine" was one of the songs Stevie had written while under his old contract with Motown and Motown had wanted to use it on *Music of My Mind*. But Stevie had refused. "It could've got lost," he explains.

Syreeta Wright had collaborated on only one of the songs on *Talking Book*, and it was one of the tracks recorded at the same time as the tracks laid down for *Music of My Mind*. After slightly over a year of marriage, the couple had concluded they were not meant to have a romantic relationship, and a few months later they separated. "Syreeta's a Leo and I'm a Taurus," Stevie explains, "our personalities were bound to explode." The two got along much better as friends and collaborators, and Stevie would produce another of her albums. Romantically, he was not alone very long. A lady named Coco was his almost constant companion on the tour to promote *Talking Book* in late 1972 and early 1973.

That tour included his debut at Carnegie Hall, and it seemed that if he could conquer that citadel of white music he had really arrived as an American star, not merely a black star. But critics often persisted in making the racial distinction.

Stevie has always said that he is first and foremost a performer, rather than a black performer. "I consider myself a performer who is . . . black," he says. So far as he was concerned he had always performed for anyone who could respond to his music, giving out love to them through his music and receiving their love in return. So it was rather irritating after the Rolling Stones tour when magazines that had either ignored him, or reviewed him as a

Stevie maintains close contact with other professional musicians and collaborates with them whenever possible, either on his records or on theirs. Roy Ayres, percussionist and leader of the group "Ubiquity" is one of the artists he respects highly. (Sue Cassidy Clark)

"black" star only, decided that Stevie Wonder was their own great discovery, as though he had not been working professionally for all those years, as though he had not had gold singles, gold albums, written songs that had been recorded by white artists, sung tunes already recorded by white singers. He sang "Blowin' in the Wind" at Carnegie Hall, and his rendition of the old effete civil rights ballad was as fresh and timely as it had been when he had first sung it as a teenager.

Meanwhile, he was hard at work on another album. When he had left Motown, it had been as if creative floodgates had opened, and his ideas continued to flow almost faster than he could capture them on tape. All those years when he had been producing formula works, his own very personal ideas had been building up in the back of his mind. A great deal of creative work gets done on a subconscious level before a note is put down on paper or tape, and Stevie had a reserve of songs that had not yet been recorded. He was impelled to share them, and though as a businessman he was aware of the conventional wisdom that it is counterproductive, indeed professionally dangerous, to release too much work at one time, he risked ruining his own market and released *Innervisions* in June 1973, barely seven months after *Talking Book*.

With *Music of My Mind* and *Talking Book*, Stevie had begun to reveal the deeper, more personal things inside his head. And with *Innervisions* he moved in even further, challenging the listener to follow him. If some of the material on *Talking Book* had been "inaccessible," most of that on *Innervisions* was downright incomprehensible to the casual listener. To understand it, one had to *work*. "*Innervisions* gives my own perspective of what's happening in my world, to my people, to all people," he said when the album was released. "That's why it took me seven months to get it together—I did all the lyrics—and that's why I think it is my most personal album. I don't care if it sells only five copies—this is the way I feel."

The flagship song on *Innervisions* was "Living for the City," and to introduce the album to the press, Stevie invited a group of journalists to go on a bus tour of New York City. When they were ready to board the bus, they found that they were to wear blindfolds for the trip, so that they could hear the city, experience it in the way that Stevie himself did, without the dazzling visual stimuli of buildings, skyline, crowds, boats on the river, all the myriad things that are New York City for the sighted. It was to be a city of sounds, shouting, laughter, traffic roaring, the fast-moving feet of the crowds, the screech of the tires, the clang of metal in a collision, the buses, the taxis, the sanitation trucks with their roaring and groaning as they choked down garbage, the clash of garbage cans, the whirr of helicopters overhead.

After they had ridden around town blindfolded for nearly an hour, to give them a sense of the physical reality of Stevie's world, they were taken to the studio to hear *Innervisions* for the first time. It had been a long time in preparation, and it was a mark of its importance to Stevie that he introduced the critics to it with such care. He had never before invited them to hear an album before it was released.

Wrote one critic, "Still in darkness [at the preview], we listened attentively, realizing the importance of this album to Stevie and his career, also aware that this is the first time we have been invited to audition any of his albums. The stuff played is heavy, and suddenly each succeeding cut sounds better. . . . Then in the stillness of my blindness, I hear a plaintive voice wailing . . . ."

(Sue Cassidy Clark)

Stevie considered "Living for the City" the most important song on the album, and he was correct in his assessment of its potential impact. For the poor, whether black or white, for all those who had experienced the bitterness and pain of poverty, the song spoke directly to their hearts. It was instantly acclaimed, sweeping the country. It was sung at fund raising events, it was mentioned in sermons, it was quoted as the ultimate statement about so many lives of so many Americans. It helped shatter the myth in so many people's minds that America was the land of plenty. The poor had always known it wasn't that, had known how hard it was to get up out of poverty. You could have plans and you could have ambitions, and you could have brains; but lack of food, long hours of poorly paid work or no work at all, bad housing, could take the soul out of genius, not to mention an average man or woman.

If "Living for the City" had expressed the essence of the experience of poverty for both blacks and whites, "All in Love Is Fair" became an instant classic for another group of people, those who had experienced the joy of love and then the agony of lost love. Indicative of its universality is the fact that both Frank Sinatra and Barbra Streisand recorded it, each in his or her own very different style, and had hits.

Stevie had taken a chance when he released *Innervisions*, for he was exposing himself more than most entertainers at that time cared to do. The title says it all. But, in retrospect, the intensely personal character of the songs is precisely why it has been so successful. David March of *Newsday* wrote of *Innervisions*, "With his last three albums, Stevie has accomplished what few rock musicians ever do. He has made one record after another which

not only seems to transcend his previous work, but also reflects a cohesive style, a unity of direction and purpose which renders comparisons of quality among the albums futile."

Had Stevie never produced another record, his three one-man albums would have assured him a place in American music history. They would have commanded respect, for themselves and for the artist who had produced them. They represented a

Stevie feels he would like to devote the bulk of his time to composing and recording, but he can still captivate a live audience better than almost anyone else in the music world. (David Ellis/*Retna)*

steady progression toward the personal/universal that many more mature artists have been unable to attain, and the climax had been reached in a comparatively short time—barely two-and-a-half years since he had left Motown. Stevie had been impelled to work that fast, obsessed with putting his ideas into tangible form, defying the traditions of the music business. Stevie explains why he felt so driven: "I felt like something was going to happen. I felt that there was going to be a change in my life. Something was going to happen that was going to be very, very significant."

To promote *Innervisions*, Stevie and his troupe went on a tour of the South. He wanted to reach southern listeners, try to communicate his message to them. But the result was disappointing. "The people couldn't feel me, and I didn't know if it was because of me, or because of the way we were presenting the show," he recalls. He is highly sensitive about his onstage performances—even egotistical about his ability to excite and relate to an audience—and when the transcendant, spiritual feeling of togetherness does not occur, he can become almost desperate. Once, during a concert in Kingston, Jamaica, before a crowd of people who were largely unfamiliar with his work and thus needed to have his greatness proven to them, a bewildered Stevie announced that he would pack up and go home if the audience wasn't having a good time. The experience in the South had him similarly worried. On the night of August 5, after a disappointing show in Greenville, South Carolina, he called a meeting with his band to talk about it. "We had to get it together, to work more together," says Stevie. "I was very upset."

The next day, Stevie and his aide, John Harris, set out from Greenville in a rented car to drive to Raleigh, North Carolina. Stevie, riding in the front seat, fell asleep not long after they had got on the highway. Harris, humming to himself as he drove along, stopped humming and frowned as he approached a logging truck, weaving from side to side on the two-lane highway. Harris moved up behind the truck preparing to pass it, when the driver suddenly slammed on his brakes. The logs jarred free, and one of them crashed through the windshield and into Stevie's skull. He was pulled from the wreck unconscious, covered with blood.

Wherever he goes, Stevie is asked to perform, and he readily obliges. (Kwame Brathwaite)

Ira Tucker, Stevie's road manager, publicist, general aide-de-camp, and friend, is never far away. Here he and Chris Jones of Motown Records Public Relations Department, discuss the next move in one of Stevie's usually busy days. (Kwame Brathwaite)

Stevie visits the Dance Theatre of Harlem, one of the many non-profit organizations he supports. Here, he treats members of the company and members of the community to a rendition of his latest songs. (Kwame Brathwaite)

Stevie joins in a song with the local dance group that has come to perform for him. (Kwame Brathwaite)

Stevie Wonder Day

Minisink Townhouse, a day care center in Harlem and one of Stevie's favorite charities, hosted a "Stevie Wonder Day" in December 1976. Among the dignitaries at the awards presentation were Percy Sutton, then the President of the Borough of Manhattan (at left) and State Senator H. Carl McCall.
(Kwame Brathwaite)

At the Museum of African Art, Frederick Douglass Institute, Washington, D.C., Stevie was honored with a party and presented with a piece of African sculpture. (Kwame Brathwaite)

The Studio Museum in Harlem invited Stevie to participate in its Children's Arts Festival in December 1976, where he inspected the work in progress of some of the young artists. (Kwame Brathwaite)

At the Studio Museum in Harlem, Stevie enjoyed the tactile qualities of an Elizabeth Catlett sculpture, then examined the sculptures of neighborhood children. (Kwame Brathwaite)

6
Rebirth

(Wide World Photos)

Whether in concert or elsewhere, sound is all around Stevie Wonder. (Jim Cummins)

Stevie Wonder lay in a coma in the intensive care unit of North Carolina Baptist Hospital in Winston-Salem. No one knew whether he would survive. If he did live, he might not come out of the coma. If he regained consciousness, he might not be the same person. Doctors were unable to ascertain exactly what damage his brain had suffered. Ira Tucker arrived at the hospital to join other family and friends in their anxious vigil. "I couldn't even recognize him," Tucker recalls. "His head was swollen up about five times normal size. And nobody could get through to him."

The distraught Tucker cast about for a way to penetrate Stevie's unconsciousness. Knowing how his friend loved to listen to loud music, he suggested that he shout into Stevie's ear, and the doctor said to go ahead and try. But Tucker got no response. The next day, he tried again. "I got right down in his ear and sang 'Higher Ground,' " he says.

"Higher Ground" deals with the idea of a second chance and suddenly Stevie's lyrics took on new meaning for Tucker and the

anxious people standing around Stevie's hospital bed. "His hand was resting on my arm," says Tucker, "and after awhile his fingers started going in time with the song. I said, yeah! Yeeaah! This dude is gonna make it!"

Stevie was in a semi-coma for seven more days, then slowly he began to recover. One of the most devastating after-effects of the accident was that he discovered that he had completely lost his sense of smell. For a sighted person this would be an inconvenience, annoying, but not tragic. But for a blind person to lose the use of any other sense is very frightening.

Stevie's hearing, for example, helps him sense obstacles by the changes in acoustics. He can pick up what a friend is saying on the telephone across a noisy crowded room, isolate the "end of the affair" conversation, pick up snatches of dialogue which may suggest a song, then quickly make a note on his cassette recorder. Then the episode may remind him of the hardships of life and love, and a whole creative emotional experience has taken place just by courtesy of that one sense, hearing. A sighted person might not even notice the man on the phone in the first place, and certainly would not pick up on the words, the sense of what he was witnessing.

For a blind person, the sense of smell can warn of danger, fire in particular, which he has no other means of knowing about. Walking into an apparently empty room, or along an apparently empty street, a blind person can sense someone standing nearby, not just by the tiny sounds of "silence" that any human being makes but by the sense of smell.

Shocked by the loss of this sense, Stevie became afraid that he might also have lost the ability to play music. He had always been able to play; ever since he was a very small child the making of music had been his world. Suppose he had the gift no longer, suppose he had lost that magical ability to be able to "find his way" even with an instrument he had never played before. Making music was like breathing for Stevie, and if he couldn't make music he would not have felt like living. The brain is still a mystery, and no one could be sure exactly how his abilities would be affected. Only time would tell.

Friends and loved ones have a way of pushing you when they think you need it. And Stevie's friends brought his clavinet to the hospital room to encourage him to try to play. For a long time he

In response to the clamor from worried fans, Stevie held a press conference in New York barely a month after his near-fatal accident. He assured reporters he was all right but said he did not expect to perform for several months. *(Wide World Photos)*

simply sat with it, afraid of finding out that something terrible had happened to his abilities. But finally, cautiously, he began to play it, and in Ira Tucker's words, "Man, you could just see the happiness spreading all over him. I'll never forget that."

It was to be a very long recuperation. There were several weeks in the hospital, bed rest, then months of inactivity while he convalesced. It was intolerable for Stevie to have to be still for so long. The excess energy that all blind people have and that they discharge by way of blindisms—in his case, the twisting of his head—were denied to Stevie during his period of convalescence. Because of the nature of his injury, it was essential that his head, normally in constant motion, be still.

But the time passed eventually, and his sense of smell returned little by little. There would be a slight permanent impairment, but not one that would seriously affect him. His wounds healed, his strength began to return. It was a period when he was forced to look inward and begin to build up a rich storehouse of music for later, when he could work again. Stevie's memory is highly developed, like his acute hearing, a sense which has been sharpened in compensation for his lack of sight. And this inner world of fantasies and memories sustained Stevie during this time, as did his conviction that the accident had been that "happening" he had foreseen.

Stevie felt that he had had a very close brush with death, that he might well have died if there had not been some higher reason for his continuing to live. His life, his music might have ended there on that Carolina road. His life had hung in the balance for three days. It had been like a rebirth, as he inched his way back, learning again how precious living was, delighting again in the sounds of the world around him, in the presence of friends and loved ones. A crisis sharpens a person's perceptions of everything around him, every bird song, the smell of the summer air, the rustle of leaves, the cold snap of fall on the way. It was not surprising that it awoke very strong religious feelings in a person whose life was based on expressions of his own spirituality and the spirituality of humankind. Since he had brought his inner world to the surface for all of his working life, made it tangible through the medium of music, it was natural that the accident, which had almost cost him his life, should have intensified his religious feelings.

It changed him a great deal. Ira Tucker says, "I've seen this dude go through a lot of changes, and I've learned a lot from him. The accident has changed him more than anything; it's really cooled him out. There was a time when if he wasn't playing the piano or singing or listening to tapes, he'd get restless and have to go out and do something, buy this or that, or go to the studio . . . something. He never used to sleep. He'd call me at four in the morning and say, 'Hey, we gotta go to the studio right now.' But I think he's over the hump now; he's got an idea of what it's all about."

Stevie pondered the mysteriousness of the event, the log like a thunderbolt turning dream to darkness. He had been asleep; then he was in another kind of sleep for several more days. "The only thing I know about it is what I read . . . I can't tell you what happened," he says. "Then I was out for four or five days so I can't tell you about that either."

He questioned those around him, those who had known what was going on when he had not. One morning he called Ira Tucker to ask, "Tuck, when I was out cold in the hospital, did I do a lot of heavy breathing?" When Tucker said he certainly had, Stevie said simply, "I thought so," and hung up. He seemed to have a need to understand, as much as he could, what had happened, to place the fragments of memory and sensation during his period in the hospital in some sort of reference frame. Having done that, he felt he could ascertain the meaning of it all.

"My outlook on life has gotten a little deeper—closer to me," he concluded. "I learned who loved me—like Abner, president of Motown, stuck with me all the way. And I learned about those who just said, 'Is he gonna be able to work again?'

"I also see that God was telling me to slow down, to take it easy. I still feel I'm here to do something for Him, to make it possible for people to communicate with each other better. And that's what I'll do. If you go by your feelings, your first impressions, they'll almost never lead you wrong. That's what I didn't do before."

Though forced to take it easy during his later convalescence, Stevie was not inactive. He went to New York after his release from the hospital, attended showings of two movies, *Detroit 9000* and *Gordon's War*, went to Buddy Mile's concert at the Schaeffer Festival in Central Park, and sat for interviews in his suite at the Fifth Avenue Hotel in Greenwich Village. Already he was planning his next album, listening to tracks that had not been included on

Since his brush with death in 1973, Stevie has become more introspective, more spiritual.
(Michael Putnam/*Retna*)

Stevie did not go on a United States concert tour until more than a year after the accident, in the fall of 1974. Singer Roberta Flack sponsored a kick-off party for it in New York in September.
(United Press International)

Music of My Mind, Talking Book and *Innervisions*. But he did not expect to begin serious work on it for some time, and he did not plan to appear on stage for another three or four months. Actually, he would return to the stage much earlier, and quite unexpectedly.

Six weeks after Stevie's release from the hospital, some friends of singer Elton John invited Stevie to attend a concert John was giving at Boston Garden. The two stars had never met, and John's friends had come up with a plan for a surprise introduction. Stevie was smuggled aboard John's private plane before it took off from the New York airport. Once in flight, John followed his usual custom and invited his guests to the lounge specially equipped with a well-stocked bar, an organ and an organist. The organist struck a few soulful chords, and John discovered his cocktail organist was Stevie Wonder. The two talked for awhile as the plane made its way into Boston, and Stevie accompanied the white star backstage at Boston Garden, where he felt John's famous neon eyeglasses. Then he took his seat out front.

When the scheduled concert was over, John obliged the cheering audience with an encore. Then he held up his hands for quiet. "A friend of mine is here," he told the audience of eighteen thousand people. "He was badly hurt in an accident some time ago . . . " The roar of the crowd interrupted him. They knew he was talking about Stevie. They applauded, they stood, and Ira Tucker led Stevie to the front of the hall and up the stairs to the stage. He and John did "Honky Tonk Woman" together. Then Stevie, the scars which he had refused to have erased through cosmetic surgery visible on his brow, launched into "Superstition." When he finished, the applause shook the building like an earthquake and the love welled up like a floodtide. Stevie Wonder was back.

Across the country, fans clamored for Stevie, but he chose to return to the stage officially not in the United States but in Europe. In January 1974 he flew to Cannes to play a twenty-minute set at MIDEM. Then he went on to Britain. He had always felt comfortable playing before British audiences. He had still not completely recovered from the accident, but he was desperate to perform again, to be assured by the roaring crowds that his talent had not been impaired. He felt he would be under less pressure in Britain.

Yolanda Simmons accompanied Stevie on that tour. Although Stevie was still legally married to Syreeta Wright (their divorce would become final in the spring of 1974), Londie, as he calls her, had been his constant companion for months. The two had met when she was looking for a job as a secretary with his New York publishing company, Black Bull. "We really met on the phone," he recalls. "I liked the way she sounded, and we became friends. Then, it turned into other feelings, which made our friendship more beautiful." Stevie now called Yolanda his fiancée, but he was in no hurry to marry again. He regretted the failure of his marriage to Syreeta, was aware of the obstacles in the path of a lasting commitment and aware of the greater obstacles presented by his stardom.

The fact that he was blind did not concern him. He knew that even for sighted persons love is too often blind. "I can usually tell about a woman by her conversation," he says. "Her voice and the way she carries herself. Some women can have a very beautiful outer face and a very ugly inner face."

But his stardom necessitated great wariness. "I used to meet girls and I'd say, 'You know me as Stevie Wonder but I want you to know me like I am. I mean, eventually I'm going to stop singing . . .' And she'd say, 'No, no, you can't stop singing!' I'd say, but my name is really Steve Morris, and she'd say, 'Yeah, but you'll always be Little Stevie Wonder to me, baby.' "

Yolanda was different, a calm strong person, not dependent on Stevie's star image. And, although she had ambition, she was not interested in being a star herself.

During the period of Stevie's convalescence, some of the personnel of Wonderlove had changed. There were two new guitarists and a new bassist. Stevie had written a new song to feature the band. Called "Contusion," its title held eerie references to Stevie's accident, in which he had suffered brain contusions, yet, in a play on words, actually referred to the meaning of the Latin root of the word, which means *beat*. Both the new band members and the new tune were introduced in Britain and, as Stevie had hoped, the audience response was excited and gratifying. Against the wishes of everyone around him, he decided to stay in Britain an extra week.

Stevie's co-workers become his close friends. He and Chris Jones of Motown Records Public Relations Department are especially close.
(Kwame Brathwaite)

The effort was almost too taxing. As one critic put it, "He couldn't get into the groove. The shows spluttered and faltered, but still his audience called him back." After the end of the regularly scheduled time of the first extra concert, he did an encore. Then the audience called for a second encore. Personally unhappy with the show and desperate not to sell his audience short, Stevie dragged himself back onstage, but he did not have the strength to do another number. So he made one of the most emotional gestures he has ever been seen to make. Geoff Brown, who witnessed it, wrote in *Melody Maker*, "He edged towards the front of the stage and took off his dark glasses—'This is the only pair I have with me,' he said—and he threw them to the audience. By that gesture he was saying, 'I've given you everything. These are about the only things I have left.' Without them, his unseeing eyes were naked for the whole hall to see. I felt like crying."

The troupe was supposed to leave London to return to New York at the end of February, but Stevie did not feel like being rushed. His concept of time has always been different from that of

most people—day and night are the same to him, so he feels no need to get up when the sun rises or go to bed when it sets. While under the watchful eye of Motown he had been forced to curb his natural inclination to tardiness, but since his independence, since becoming his own boss, he had allowed it free rein. At times it seemed to his harried staff that his lateness had become more of a problem since the accident. It took him three days to get himself and his belongings together enough to fly back to New York. "One thing you can depend on with Stevie is that he'll always be late. That's his way of doing things," Ira Tucker sighs. "But you just have to go with it."

Stevie and his entourage arrived back in the United States for the annual Grammy awards presentation on March 2. He had been nominated before, but never in so many categories. In January, he had made history of a sort by being nominated for six

Steve and "Londie" as he calls Yolanda Simmons, met on the telephone. "I can usually tell about a woman from her conversation," he says. (Kwame Brathwaite)

In January 1974, Stevie made music history when he was nominated for an unprecedented six Grammys. At the presentation ceremonies in March, he enjoyed a virtual one-man sweep of the awards, capturing four of them. Singer Alice Cooper was one of the presenters. *(Wide World Photos)*

Grammys, more than any other artist in the sixteen-year history of the awards, and industry gossip had it that he would win more than one of the music business's equivalent of the Oscar. He made sure most of his family was there, and proudly escorted his mother. Mrs. Hardaway sat happily beside her son as he enjoyed a virtual one-man sweep of the 1974 Grammy presentations.

It was a fitting climax to a progression. He had taken over the radio, taken over the discos. Now he took over the Grammys. He won five of the six awards for which he had been nominated. He accepted four: Best Pop Vocal Performance by a Male Singer ("You Are the Sunshine of My Life."), Best Pop Vocal Performance ("Superstition"), Best Rhythm and Blues Single ("Superstition"), and the top award, Album of the Year (*Innervisions*). He gave the fifth award, Best Engineered

Recording ("Superstition") to his engineers, Robert Margouleff and Malcolm Cecil.

Four times he was led up to the stage to accept the small gilded victrolas. Four times the hall rang with thunderous applause. The first time, he introduced on television the members of his family, his mother, brothers Milton and Calvin, and his twelve-year-old sister, Renee. The next three times he groped for something to say. The audience laughed with him—after all, how many prepared acceptance speeches could one man have? He said it all when he accepted the award for Best Pop Vocal Performance by a Male Singer: "I would like to thank you all for making this the sunshine of my life tonight."

(United Press International)

No other artist had ever won as many Grammys in one year. There could no longer be any doubt that Stevie Wonder was a major musical talent. Only three years before he had forced Motown to give him a contract that would guarantee his musical independence. Motown benefited, too, from the Grammys Stevie had won. Indeed, just as he had put the old Hitsville U.S.A. on its feet with the success of "Fingertips," Stevie had helped open up the Motown label to the white rock audience, delivered, as one writer put it, their last underdeveloped market. With Marvin Gaye, who had also demanded an independent relationship with Motown and been successful, Stevie had done much to maintain the importance of Motown in the record world after Berry Gordy had turned his attention increasingly to motion pictures. "I'm unashamed to say Stevie and Marvin changed our approach," said Ewart Abner, president of Motown Records. "They loosened us up. We make a lot of money and we didn't have to change. They taught us how to have a little fun." Both artists had defied the traditional company formulas and shown they were right not only artistically but in the business sense as well.

Stevie would win other awards that year, but they would not particularly please him. Not one of the titles of his Grammy awards had contained the word *soul*, and as it was a categorization that he often railed against, he could see only regression in the award from the National Association of Record Merchandisers, which named him best-selling soul artist of the year, and in the American Music awards for best male soul vocalist and best soul single.

"I kinda feel," he sighs, "that after writing all those songs like 'All in Love Is Fair' and 'Visions,' well, that to say I'm just a soul artist is

***Overleaf:* On March 26, 1974, Stevie gave a concert at Madison Square Garden in New York. It was his first concert appearance in the United States since the accident, and the fans greeted him with an almost religious fervor.**
(Kwame Brathwaite)

wrong because all those songs are typical ballads of America. I am a black man, but music is music. I want to be an inspiration to my people, but I don't want to be categorized." And he was well aware that honors can become labels. In his opinion, using the word *soul* is like putting *super* in front of everything.

Stevie still had not given an American concert since his accident, and in late March he had planned to launch a five-week, twenty-city tour with a concert at Madison Square Garden. But two weeks before he cancelled all the dates after New York. "I didn't do the tour because there was no concept to it," he explained. "I was disgusted with the whole thing. People were always coming to me saying, 'Steve, Steve, Steve . . . ' I said let's leave it alone for a while, until everything cools down. I want to do other things now—to have children and to do as much as I can for my people." He honored his commitment to the date at Madison Square Garden partly because he felt he should return to the American concert stage (the clamor to see him had increased), partly because after appearing at the Garden with the Stones two years earlier he was returning to the same hall as a headliner, and partly because he had already promised some of the proceeds to the Minisink Town House, a Harlem organization for disadvantaged children. He let his staff deal with the furor caused by the other cancellations. Before the accident, he would not have taken this step. Now he had decided he did not have to accede to any but self-engendered pressure. Although he still enjoyed performing, his heart was in the recording studio.

For that one night at Madison Square Garden, however, his heart was with the audience, and their hearts were with him. In a way, he had become for the seventies what Bob Dylan had been in the sixties, a star who had looked death in the face and said, "Not yet." There was a special aura about him in the eyes of the twenty thousand people who packed the Garden that night. As Robert Christgau wrote in the *Village Voice*, "The only act who could have topped Stevie Wonder was Jesus Christ. He had come close enough to dying the previous summer to make a lot of us realize how much we hoped of him, and then proceeded to surge across the radio to his sweep of the Grammys, when the record business finally acknowledged a small part of its debt to black music. The Garden was his victory celebration."

The "Contusion" number, first introduced to British audiences

The party to kick off Stevie's tour was held at Delmonico's. Mick Jagger of the Rolling Stones attended and wished Stevie well. It had been two years since Stevie had accompanied the Stones on their U.S. tour, and Stevie was now as well known as they were. *(United Press International)*

and never before seen by an American crowd, had been extended to a half-hour segment, divided into "Approaching Contusion" and "Contusion." During that time, each of the musicians on stage was introduced by Stevie, sitting at the three-tier construct of instruments, the ARP synthesizer. For the next seventy-five minutes, however, the show was almost entirely Stevie, paced and shaped as only he could do it. He began with familiar songs and steadily built the momentum to the climax, an extended, dancelike version of "Living for the City." Two songs later, he took the mood down again, to build up excitement for the finale. Roberta Flack, Sly Stone and Eddie Kendricks were all invited to join Stevie in a rousing rendition of "Superstition." Sly tried to steal the show by slipping in a loud "Higher," but Stevie grasped him firmly by the hand and showed him to the wings; this was his night alone.

The presence of all four artists on the stage of Madison Square Garden was significant. It stressed the increasingly strong claim of black music to a central position in American popular music. The audience cheering the show's finale was as thoroughly integrated as an audience could be. There were no encores, but no one in the audience seemed to mind. Wrote Christgau, "The sweet spirit of the concert, in all its integrated optimism, was like a one-night Summer of Love. The next day, everything looked like 1974 again, but for a brief time we could feel our power to defeat our own death wish."

Now it was time for Stevie to return to the recording studios to work on his album. He'd not been a stranger to the studios all those months since the release of *Innervisions*. In the interim he had produced Syreeta's second album, *Stevie Wonder Presents Syreeta*, which would be far more successful than her first. As collaborators, the two were highly compatible. "Stevie sends me the rhythm and the tune, I work on the lyrics, and then he either approves or we discuss it further," she explained on the occasion of her New York debut later that year. Syreeta was not the only artist he had helped or would help. He was also producing an album by his band, Wonderlove. While still at Motown, he had produced the Spinners recording, "It's a Shame," a Christmas song with the Miracles, Smokey Robinson's "We Had a Love So Strong," tunes with David Ruffin and Martha Reeves, with the Jackson Five and the Osmond Brothers. Among the songs he wrote and produced for the Jackson Five was "No News Is Good

News." "It's a tune I did during the English tour," says Stevie. "I was going to do it myself, but there was a party for me after the Grammy awards, and I played it, and the Jackson Five said right there they wanted to do it. The Osmonds wanted to do it, too. It was really funny, like a tug of war."

He would help produce Minnie Ripperton's first album, but Motown would not allow him to receive credit for this "outside production work." Rufus, the rhythm and blues band, would win a Grammy for "Tell Me Something Good," released in the summer of 1974, whose music Stevie had written. In early February, Aretha Franklin's recording of "Until You Come Back to Me (That's What I'm Gonna Do)" was at the top of the "soul" charts. The song had been written by Stevie, Clarence Paul and Mo Broadmax *thirteen years* earlier. Stevie had worked on over-dubbing with Eric Clapton. As *Melody Maker* predicted in January 1974, "... expect a firmer move into production of other acts."

But though Stevie enjoyed collaborating with and helping out his fellow artists, when he had something to say musically he wanted to get at it. The new album was scheduled for release in a month, and it was still, in his opinion, in the rough stage. Tentatively, it was to be a double album, titled *Fulfilling Ness's First Finale*. It would contain the tracks not used on the three earlier albums and would, as Stevie hoped the title would suggest, close out the first period in his life.

April came and went and the album was still not ready. To the uninitiated, it might have seemed that Stevie was just noodling around with it, for all the tracks had been laid down. But Stevie is a perfectionist when it comes to music. There were still rough spots, he felt, problems to work out, chords or lyrics that did not sound quite right. He would not allow to be issued any recording with which he was not completely satisfied.

Motown knew better than to try to push him. The company had learned that Stevie had an exquisite musical sense, and if the orders were coming in and there was no product with which to fill them, the company knew the customers would wait, and that the final product would be worth the waiting. "Higher Ground" had been pronounced gold, and the shiny disc was presented to Stevie by Ewart Abner at a party held at Los Angeles' Speakeasy Club to celebrate Stevie's twenty-fourth birthday. It brought his gold singles to a total of thirteen. He had two gold albums (*Innervisions*,

Music of My Mind), a platinum album (*Talking Book*), and a platinum single ("Superstition"). Judging from advance orders, the new album would be gold at least, so no one was unduly rushing Stevie Wonder.

When the album was released at last in late August, it was not a double album as originally planned. And the title had been changed to *Fulfillingness' First Finale*, perhaps because of the possible confusion with the Loch monster. Playing the tape the morning after the final mix had been completed, Stevie was satisfied. "It's very important that you concentrate on the lyrics," he said. "I feel very peaceful inside for the first time." He made an obvious reference to Yolanda. "Things change when you meet someone that is very positive and gives you peace and understanding far better than any relationship in the past." He felt no sense of urgency now. Although he planned to release the second part of the album, he thought he might wait quite a while to do so. "Then," he said, "I might wait a long time, maybe more than a year after the second record, before I release another album. The title indicates that this is the last of this kind of stuff that I'll be doing—different songs and essentially the same instrumentation. I think my next thing might be largely orchestral, a long piece."

Although the album was shipped with orders worth almost two million dollars and was the nation's best-selling LP by September 1974, it was not as well received by critics as the two previous albums. Some complained about lyrics, finding them "gushy," "sentimental." Joseph Mills wrote in the New York *Times*, "Stevie is a genius, but his taste is moving too far into the mystic and the romantic for me."

Other critics took the album to be a reflection of Stevie's feelings about the "message" of the accident and explained the mystical and philosophical aspects of many of the songs within that framework. Actually, most of the songs had been written before the accident, and there was really no departure from the style or content of *Talking Book* or *Innervisions*, but perhaps if the accident had not forced Stevie to slow down, he might have done so anyway. He had reached a time in his life when he felt he must slow down, reflect on himself, on his purpose and direction in life. *Fulfullingness' First Finale* is an introspective album, but then, from *Music of My Mind* through *Innervisions* Stevie had been growing progressively more introspective in his music. Accident

Stevie won the Grammy for Best Album of the Year for *Fulfillingness' First Finale* at the 17th annual awards ceremony in March 1975. The award was presented to him by singer Bette Midler, who adorned her hair with a 45 rpm disc for the occasion. *(United Press International)*

or no accident, this was the direction in which he seemed to be going, and it is perhaps more accurate to view the album as representing Stevie at a particular time of his life and career, rather than Stevie affected by his brush with death.

Even the critics who complained about the lyrics had nothing but fulsome praise for the album musically. It was rich with musical treasures, another display of Stevie's dazzling multiple talents, and another collection of something for everyone. With "You Haven't Done Nothing" he moved further into political expression. The most militant song he had ever produced, it denounced empty liberal promises of righting the wrongs in the world. Previously, Stevie had always been cautious in dealing in his music with his situation as a black man in America. But by 1974 his position was such that when he spoke out he spoke from a position of high achievement, high visibility, and he was listened to. This is not to say the lyrics were exactly Black Power rhetoric; the song may have been militant for Stevie, but it was comparatively tame. It is perhaps noteworthy that the Jackson Five sings backup vocal on the song. In the course of the song, the quintet of young black men is exhorted by name to "sing it loud for your people." "I didn't necessarily do it because of that," says Stevie, "but after I did, I felt I would like them to be identified with more than nyah-nyah-nyah-nyah-nyah. But I would've liked the Osmonds on the record, too. I think they [the two groups, one black, one white] could really bring people together." The cut, which featured the driving electronic "do wop" rhythm so successfully employed in "Superstition," became a hit single.

"They Won't Go When I Go," on the other hand, might appeal to lovers of classical music. Musical influences can lie fallow for years in a composer's mind, and the emergence of the influences of the music of Bach and Chopin, which Stevie had learned to play years earlier at the Michigan School for the Blind, is evident in this cut. It sounds almost like a musical exercise and is undoubtedly a result of Stevie's hearing of "Switched-On Bach" back in 1971 and his desire to try a similar rendition of classical forms on the electronic synthesizer.

He further revealed his command of the synthesizer in "It Ain't No Use," which incorporated various musical tracks, background vocalizing by Wonderlove and the Persuasions, and his own voice in a richly patterned texture.

Never before had his own voice emerged so much like a musical instrument itself. He ranged from Louis Armstrong-like growls, to a blues wail, to a soft calypso croon. There is even a bossa nova number, "Bird of Beauty." "Boogie on Reggae Woman," a song that bears little resemblance to the Jamaican style but is highly sensuous, became another hit single thanks to the disco craze; and there is a very religious song, "Heaven is Ten Zillion Light Years Away." Of all the lyrics, those on this song are perhaps the most awkward and unimaginative. Some critics felt this album might signal the peaking of Stevie's proselytizing period. They were wrong. More likely, the awkwardness of the lyrics on "Heaven" simply indicated Stevie's (man's) inability to express cosmic feelings.

(Kwame Brathwaite)

Although he had tired of "running up and down the road," as he put it, he was aware that across the country there was a tremendous desire to see him on the part of the fans, and the release of *Fulfillingness'* was an obvious reason for a national tour. He did not mind doing a tour that had "a concept" behind it. It would be the first tour for his new band, for which he had screened nearly two hundred musicians. He had not felt the former Wonderlove had been in total synch with him. Only one guitarist, Michael Sembello, had been retained. The new band would deliver his music, as one writer put it, "with all its delicate color intact." He opened the tour in mid-September with a concert at Long Island's Nassau Coliseum and, thirty-five cities full of packed houses later, closed with a Christmas concert at Madison Square Garden whose proceeds would be donated to charity.

For Stevie, it was among his most enjoyable tours because he refused to let the pressure get to him. He had taken to going to the nearest park in whatever city he was in and spending time there, sitting amid the trees, listening to the sound of the new place, enjoying a solitude and peace away from the pressures of scheduling and lining up equipment and setting up sound systems and too many people around.

His staff did not mind. They were paid to see to such things, and everyone knew Stevie was doing a lot of thinking lately. But they did wish he shared their concept of time. Somehow, every scheduled concert was given, but there were some gut-tightening moments. Ira Tucker remembers the time in Detroit: "Steve was forty-five minutes late in going on or something. Everybody's going

Stevie enjoyed being on the road in the United States again, taking his music directly to the audience. His band was almost entirely new now, and the tour had a "concept" to it, which was very important to him. (Sue Cassidy Clark)

crazy, you know, having heart attacks because Steve is just sitting in the dressing room trying to get his hair to look right. But I wasn't worried. I said listen, folks, there's no problem here; no reason to panic. After all, Steve was *in* the place; eventually he'd go on and then everything's cool."

And then there was the particularly harrying time in Seattle two weeks later. "Steve is due to go on in thirty minutes," Tucker remembers with a shudder, "the only hangup being that nobody's

seen Steve since the day before. Suddenly, as the tension mounts, the phone rings. Guess who? Steve! He was calling from L.A. to say he missed the plane. Missed the *plane*. And he's supposed to be onstage in *thirty minutes*. Man, that one just blew a lot of people away. And I said, okay . . . *now* we have a problem. *Now* anybody who wants to panic can go right ahead. . . . That is life with Steve."

Once onstage, Stevie frequently spent considerable time warming up, getting into the groove. He showed his independence further by dispensing with renditions of some of his past hits and performing instead songs that had been hits for other artists, songs like the Penguins' "Earth Angel," the Temptations' "Ain't Too Proud to Beg," Gladys Knight's "I Heard It Through the Grapevine." And he spent more time "rapping" to the audience, introducing his band, promoting various charities. Many in the audience would grow restless, making it necessary for Stevie to say, too often, "For those of you that are talking . . . relax your lips." He would talk about "pure love between all people," regardless of race, and the audience would try to applaud enthusiastically. But this was a concert in the 1970s, not a 1960s love-in. The sentiments rang hollow to many, and Stevie knew it. "I hear that so many of you may clap when I talk about what I'm talking about," he told the audience at the final concert at Madison Square Garden. "But unfortunately the only place where I find this love that I talk about is in my dreams, in the songs that I write . . . " The audience would shift uncomfortably in their seats.

Then Stevie would launch into a song, and express the same sentiments, and the audience would fall out of their seats cheering. The lesson: They could take the preaching, if it was put to a good beat. Perhaps that is one reason why Stevie has come to prefer recording to performing.

Once the tour ended, Stevie returned in earnest to the New York recording studios. He'd changed his mind about the second part of *Fulfillingness' First Finale*; he wanted to issue it right away. "Otherwise," he explained, "it's going to have to wait almost another year—and I'm going to want to be doing some other stuff by then."

He was advised not to do it, "Right on the heels of a smash, you want to release it?" asked Ira Tucker incredulously. *Talking Book* had been on the charts almost three years. *Fulfillingness'* was on. Did he really want three of his albums competing with each other for sales? Stevie did not care about sales. He wanted to finish up that period of his life, go on to new things. In the end, however, the conventional wisdom prevailed. No *Fulfillingness' Last Finale* or *Further Fulfillingness'* was forthcoming. Although some of the material would be included on his next album, it would be a year and a half before the world would be treated to a new offering by Stevie Wonder.

"I know now that music shouldn't be so important to me that I

don't do the important things of life," Stevie had said one day not long after his accident, and in early 1975 he attended to some of those "important things." Yolanda was pregnant. "I've always wanted to be a father," says Stevie. "But I knew I had to wait till I met the right woman who would give my child the love it needs." They had once considered marriage, but now had apparently decided against it. "Love is free—it's not about possession," Stevie explains. It was time, however, to put down some roots, to quit the hotel scene.

On January 2, 1975, they went to look at the Civil War-period brownstone home of the chairman of the board of a major New

Aisha, just over one month old, attends with her parents a luncheon given by the Congressional Black Caucus in the Rayburn Office Building, Washington, D.C., and is introduced by Representative Ronald Dellums of California. (Kwame Brathwaite)

Aisha is introduced to a local dog—a day in the country represents a variety of new experiences for her. (Kwame Brathwaite)

One nice thing about having a famous Daddy is being able to meet the clowns at the Ringling Brothers Barnum & Bailey Circus. For Stevie Wonder, one of the nice things about life is having a three-year-old daughter named Aisha. *(Wide World Photos)*

York publisher. Yolanda liked the antique brass chandeliers and marble bathrooms, the cherry paneling from Vermont; Stevie put to rest the seller's and the neighbors' fears of loud music at night by promising to soundproof the top floor as a studio; and within a month the deal was consummated. The man who had stolen coal to keep warm as a little boy plunked down $175,000 cash for his new home. They moved in the next month.

March came and with it the annual Grammy awards. Once again, it was The Stevie Wonder Show, for once again he won five awards, sweeping the major categories: Best Album of the Year, as artist, for *Fulfillingness' First Finale* (so much for the lyric-conscious critics); Best album of the Year, as producer; Best Pop Male Vocalist; Best R&B Male Vocal Performance for the single "Boogie on Reggae Woman"; Best R&B Song. Once again, the audience laughed with Stevie as he struggled to come up with something new to say on each trip to the podium. The result was a rather strange mix. As writer O'Connell Driscoll commented, "Anyone who can stand up on national television and accept a Grammy award in the memory of Elijah Muhammad and Jack Benny can do anything at all."

What pleased Stevie most that spring, however, was not what he alone could do—win five Grammy awards for the second year in a row—but what any healthy man can do, become a father. On April 7, 1975, while Stevie stalked the corridors of the maternity ward at St. Luke's hospital in Manhattan, Yolanda gave birth to an eight-pound girl. She was named Aisha Zakia, a combination of African words for strength and intelligence, and she would be, for Stevie, "the sunshine of my life." He would understand her gurgling sounds, discern her different cries, perceive her in ways no one else could. He would include a cut on his next album called "Isn't She Lovely," devoted to the sounds his tiny daughter made in the bath.

7

Higher Ground

By the spring of 1975 the recording industry was rife with rumors that Stevie Wonder was the subject of a bidding war among Motown, Epic and Arista Records. His three-year contract with Motown was up and it was known he was unhappy with some of the provisions it had contained. He wanted, for example, to produce artists on other labels, and the Jackson Five, who had left Motown to sign with Epic, had approached him about producing them on their new label. He also wanted to be able to choose which album cuts were released as singles—the "Superstition" misunderstanding still rankled. Moreover, it was known that he was unhappy with the Motown plan to release an album called *Stevie Wonder Anthology*. It would include his biggest hits and would fill the void between *Fulfillingness' First Finale* and Stevie's next album, which was nowhere near completion. In Motown's opinion, that was good business. In Stevie's opinion, it was bad art. Musically, he had gone beyond his earlier hits. He enjoyed doing them in concert, but he did not want them re-recorded and re-released. Anyway, he did not feel the collection represented

1975—Performing before a Jamaican audience largely unfamiliar with his music, Stevie went all-out to win them. He takes audience reactions very personally and equates a lack of enthusiasm for his music as a lack of enthusiasm for him.
(Kwame Brathwaite)

25

a true history of his music.

Would Stevie leave Motown over these disagreements? If he did, said some, it would signal the demise of Motown Records. The company's roster of artists had diminished steadily over the last few years. Diana Ross, the Temptations, Smokey Robinson and Marvin Gaye had remained, but though they were big stars they were also older stars. Whatever new blood had been infused lately had been siphoned off by other record companies. Berry Gordy, the genius at spotting young musical talent, seemed to have become preoccupied with film production at the expense of the record company. Without Stevie Wonder, Motown would no longer be a major force in the music field.

There was a period of intensive negotiation, yet Stevie never seriously considered leaving the company. He knew what his leaving would mean to Motown. He felt he owed it something. "If it were not for Motown, many of us just wouldn't have had the shot we've had at success and fulfillment," he said later. He also remembered the aftermath of his accident, how he had found out who his friends really were, and how Motown Record's president, Ewart Abner, had been one of them. He wanted to stay with Motown, but he wanted to re-sign with the company on his own terms. He got most of them. The contract signed between Stevie Wonder and Motown Records on August 5, 1975, was unprecedented in the freedom granted the artist. It also involved more money than had ever been paid to any music superstar before.

"I knew we weren't prepared to offer that kind of money," said a spokesman for Arista, after hearing that Stevie would be guaranteed an income of more than $13 million over the next seven years. Music industry bosses also shuddered at Wonder's new 20%+ royalty rate (the usual superstar rate is 12-15%). But the money was not all. Stevie Wonder would be allowed to produce artists on other labels "to a prescribed degree"; he would have the right to choose which of his songs would be issued as singles; *and* he had won the right to suppress the controversial and much publicized *Stevie Wonder Anthology* album. According to industry sources, that part of the agreement meant that Motown would have to destroy two hundred thousand copies that had already been pressed.

In return, Motown got . . . Stevie Wonder. But, in the view of the

Whether onstage in a small auditorium, or on an outdoor platform before an audience that extends for miles, Stevie can command the attention of his listeners like no other performer. (Kwame Brathwaite)

In ceremonies at the Sheraton-Park Hotel in Washington, D.C., Stevie was presented with an award for his support of the principles of human kindness. At left are Carol Kirkendall and Darrell Brooks, organizers of Human Kindness Day. At right are Representative Ronald Dellums of California and Ewart Abner, president of Motown Records. (Kwame Brathwaite)

A celebration of Human Kindness Day was held in Washington, D.C., in May 1975. Stevie, an apostle of human kindness, was the special honoree. Thousands attended his free concert in front of the Washington Monument in the most peaceful gathering of such magnitude the city has ever seen. *(Wide World Photos)*

company, it was a good deal. "He's the premier artist, composer, performer of the day and he should have the best contract," said Abner.

He was also the premier artist/businessman.

Of all the terms of the contract, Stevie considered those involving money least important. He'd been after artistic control, and he'd got it. "My life is not about money," he says, and for someone who makes as much money as he does, he lives quite modestly. He purchased a five-bedroom home for his mother and younger siblings in the San Fernando Valley, maintains an apartment in L.A. and the home in New York, but his only real extravagances are electronic equipment—his synthesizers and tape records with which he has furnished the top floor studio in his Manhattan home—and long-distance telephone calls.

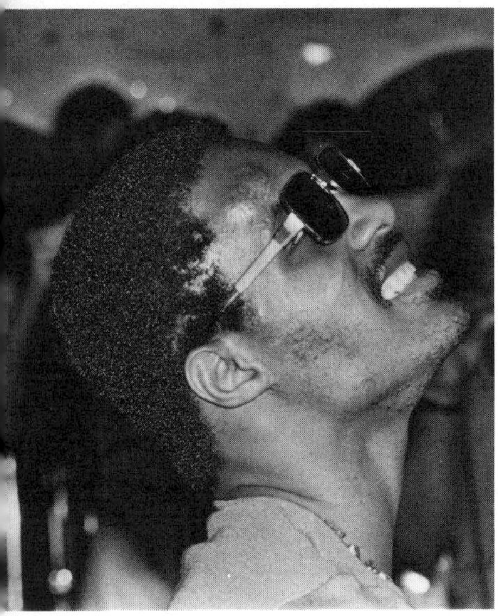

Parties and more parties. At a party *before* the surprise birthday party for Stevie on the Human Kindness Day weekend, Stevie revels in the sounds and the bustle of activity.
(Kwame Brathwaite)

He is extremely generous. He pays the salaries of his studio and touring musicians and singers whether they work or not. "How many cats'll do that?" asks one, who is aware that it is customary in the music world to pay touring musicians only for the duration of the tour or studio singers only when a record is being cut. He also does a sizeable number of benefits for charities he considers worthwhile.

He did his share that year, 1975. In May, he served as Special Honoree at a celebration of Human Kindness Day, giving a free concert to fifty thousand people massed at the Washington Monument. In June he gave a benefit performance in San Francisco for the National Newspapers Scholarship Fund one day and sang in New York on Geraldo Rivera's annual One-to-One Telethon, donating several thousand dollars as well, the next. At Shaw University in Raleigh, North Carolina, where he is a trustee, he set up several scholarships and funded an elaborate sound system. In October, construction began on the Stevie Wonder Home for Blind and Retarded Children, scheduled to open the next spring in St. Albans, Queens, New York. Part of the program operated by the One-to-One foundation, it is a small residence facility housing twelve children. From time to time he spoke of going to Africa to help the victims of drought and to raise money for a cause that particularly concerns him, finding a way to restore the eyesight of people blinded by fungus-carrying flies and to eradicate the flies. He managed to give several concerts at penal institutions. Otherwise, he did comparatively little performing.

He was spending as much time as he could at home with Yolanda and Aisha. He delights in his child. "I can sense Yolanda and me in her," he says. "Like me, she is inquisitive about the way things work. I'd like twenty-four kids, a whole bunch, but I don't know if I'll ever make that." But as the months wore on he spent most of his time in Los Angeles, leaving Yolanda to take care of Aisha and to pursue her own interests—TM and fashion design, in which she took classes four days a week. He was working on a new album and this one, he was determined, would be a double. By the summer of 1975 he was thinking of calling it *Thank You for Letting Me into Your Home*, but no one was banking on it. He had rarely ended up with the same album title he'd started with. He was also hoping to release it in the fall, but no one was counting on that either. He had been know to spend up to ten hours on a three-second call-letter radio spot.

Fall came and went and no album materialized. Not a few people in the music industry were grateful. At the Grammy awards in

When you are a star, you are given many birthday parties. As Human Kindness Day just happened to fall near Stevie's twenty-fifth birthday, its organizers also organized a surprise birthday party for him. His mother, Mrs. Lulu Hardaway, helped him cut the cake. (Kwame Brathwaite)

March 1976, Stevie, not having released a record in 1975, was not nominated in a single category. Paul Simon won the award for best album. In accepting it, Simon thanked Stevie Wonder for not making an album in 1975.

Stevie then decided to release the album, and actually made an announcement to this effect, during the time when the sun would be in Taurus (April 21-May 21), as the "vibes" would be positive with his birth chart; but by the time of the Grammy awards presentation that date was highly doubtful as well. He had started with two hundred works, both on tape and in the "recorder of his mind." He hadn't pared down the material nearly enough. There was so much he had to say, and he was constantly creating more ways to say it.

Sought out by children wherever he goes, Stevie, with Chris Jones of Motown Records Public Relations Department, talks to a group of young Washington, D.C. fans. (Kwame Brathwaite)

Stevie in concert in Kingston, Jamaica, October 1975. Release of the album that would be called *Songs in the Key of Life* was expected that fall, but it would not materialize for another year. Stevie was the only person not worried over the delay. (Kwame Brathwaite)

He crisscrosses the country, by car, by air, and in any place at any time of the night or day, a song may come to him, words that bend themselves to a melody. He says that "usually what happens is that the melody comes first and then sometime later I'll write the lyrics. If I have my tape recorder on my piano I'll put it down on the cassette, just the melody. If I'm in the studio and I come up with something spontaneously, I'll just put down the rhythm track, which consists usually of the Moog programmed for the bass part, and the piano or clavinet or whatever I'm using. Then later I'll add the other instruments, the horns and strings and all. When the song is almost complete, that's when I'll lay down the true lyrics. It's the last thing but I will have been thinking about lyrics all along. I'll maybe come up with a punch line and then work around that theme . . . certain weeks you can write and then the next week you can't do nothin'. It's an involuntary movement. But you can't be getting worried when it doesn't come."

That, of course, was not his problem in 1975-76. His problem was harnessing the creative flow, selecting the songs and working with them until he could do no more; somehow reducing the vast amount of material to a manageable size. He could well have done a four-record album, but it would have been priced out of the reach of most record buyers, and it would have taken close to four years given his chronic perfectionitis. The clamor for the new album had begun. The pressure built.

"There were times," recalls bassist Nathan Watts, "when he'd stay in the studio forty-eight hours straight. You couldn't even get the cat to stop and eat." While those around him dropped like flies

from fatigue, Stevie worked compulsively on. "If my flow is goin', I keep on until I peak," he says simply. His harried public relations people, bombarded by urgent requests for a firm date, decided at one point to give themselves, and Stevie, a four-month leeway. At least they knew what the album would be called. Stevie had decided the title would be *Songs in the Key of Life*.

The huge, 60-by-240-foot advertisement went up in early May, a gigantic reminder that it was actually coming—a new album by Stevie Wonder, his most ambitious undertaking yet. But when? The summer wore on, and by mid-August Stevie's publicists were getting worried. They had rented the billboard until September 1. A movie advertisement was scheduled to replace it. Hasty negotiations ensued, and the space was re-rented for as long as necessary.

Late in September, seventy-six members of the press were transported to a farm in New England to hear the album before it was released. The 145-acre Long View Farm outside Worcester, Massachusetts, is rented exclusively to rock groups and is equipped with everything from complete recording facilities to a stable and thoroughbred horses. Stevie, dressed in a cowboy outfit, explained he had chosen the sylvan setting because it was appropriate to the music on his album, a reflective collection of songs about his life and his dreams. "I hope you enjoy this," he said. "But it really doesn't matter. I gave it my all and all is the best I can do."

The final product consisted of two long-playing records plus an additional seven-inch 33-rpm disc containing four songs, plus a twenty-four page booklet with all lyrics and credits. The total of twenty-one songs made it one of the longest pop albums in history, and though it had taken a seemingly endless time to be realized, it took no time at all to reach the top of the charts. One week after its release the first week of October (just before the cutoff date for 1976 Grammy eligibility), it was Number One, the fastest climb ever for a double LP. No wonder.

Stevie took time out to have some food during the long day of album autographing and answering questions about his new album. (Richard E. Aaron)

Most works anticipated with such excitement, whose release was accompanied by such brouhaha, would inevitably have been a letdown in actuality. And then there was the matter of the sheer magnitude of the work. As one critic wrote, "Double albums often indicate a failure of self-discipline more than an abundance of things to say." But these apprehensions proved groundless.

In September 1977 Stevie flew in from California to help the mayoral campaign of Manhattan Borough President Percy Sutton. Stevie wrote a song especially for the Sutton campaign, "Stand Up, Light Up, Let Your Light Shine," which the crowd, candles in hand, sang along with him. *(United Press International)*

Musically and conceptually, *Songs in the Key of Life* was a tour de force.

It did indeed seem to contain much personal history. "I Wish" voices longing for the carefree days of childhood. "Knocks Me off My Feet" is about first love; "Summer Soft" about lost love; "Ordinary Pain" about love gone bad. He celebrates the joys of music, at the same time paying tribute to his musical roots, in "Sir Duke."

It included characteristic preachifying on the themes that have been consistently part of Wonder's mature work—social justice for blacks and for the poor, faith, love among all people—in, among other cuts, "Village Ghetto Land," "Love's in Need of Love Today," "Black Man," and "Have a Talk with God." The range of subject matter is mammoth.

So is the musical territory covered. The very first cut, "Love's in Need of Love Today," appears to feature Stevie's voice backed by a gospel-type choir, until one realizes that the choir consists entirely of taped overdubs of Stevie's own voice. As usual, Stevie operates as a one-man music company—composer, singer, instrumentalist, producer. The music ranges from the Beatlesque string quartet sound of "Village Ghetto Land" to the jazz boogying of "Sir Duke," from the classical strains of "Pastime Paradise" to the pounding Brazilian drums of "Another Star." Although he is backed on a few cuts by Herbie Hancock on piano and George Benson on guitar, Stevie, one feels, did not need them and was merely continuing his habit of including friends in his work. He could have done it all, and very nearly did anyway. "There is simply no more brilliant texturalist of pop sound than Stevie Wonder," wrote Stephen Holder in *Hi Fidelity Magazine*. "One doesn't listen so much to the sound of particular instruments as to the overall fabric, which blends multiple keyboards, bass, drums, percussion, and backup vocals into seething, bursting textures that are the Stevie Wonder signature."

"Seething," "bursting"—these words and words like them constantly come to mind as one listens to the album. There is an exuberance about the album, a spontaneity, a jumping jamboree quality about it that is irresistible. Wonder may have decided not to call it *Thank You for Letting Me into Your Home*, but the album is indeed an open invitation to delight in music with the same joyous abandon with which he makes music. Despite the intervening years, this is the same Stevie who played his heart out in "Fingertips," still having the time of his life. Said Robert Christgau in the *Village Voice, Songs in the Key of Life* is Stevie Wonder's fulfillingness."

The album is not without flaws. One critic wrote, "He seems to lack any intellectual screening process for his own ideas, and as a result much of the material on *Songs in the Key of Life* would not be missed had it been left off the album." "Black Man" seems particularly out of place in a 1970s album, and out of context with the rest of the material. Other cuts are not especially memorable. But those that are will stay in the mind forever—a riff here, a lyric there, the exultant feeling of a song like "Sir Duke." There is something for everyone on this album, and almost everyone likes it. There is no doubt that it is *the* album of the seventies. Other pop albums, even the best, seem to pall in comparison, to come across as rather tame.

At the third annual Rock Music Awards in September 1977 Stevie won two "Rockies" for Male Vocalist of the Year and Best Rhythm and Blues Album for *Songs in the Key of Life*. It is his custom, when accepting awards, to remember others, and at this ceremony he gave a special salute to the late Elvis Presley. *(United Press International)*

In March 1977, fresh from an ambitious concert tour to promote *Songs*, Stevie was once again accorded the highest praise the music industry gives, this time to the power of four. His Grammys for Album of the Year, Best Male Pop Performer, Best Male Rhythm and Blues Performer and Best Producer brought his total to fourteen—in four years—and he was still only twenty-six years old.

What lies ahead for Stevie Wonder? Musically, it would seem he can only get better. The first black musician to make serious use of the synthesizer, he is the only musician to have succeeded in using it consistently without gimmickry. He is credited with almost singlehandedly bringing the synthesizer into the mainstream of popular music and is expected to continue using it to revitalize the form. Who knows what heights he can attain with this electronic marvel? The synthesizer is still a relatively new development and is constantly being improved and refined. In *Songs*, Stevie employed a Yamaha synthesizer and currently he is involved in even deeper explorations into electronic music with yet more sophisticated equipment. He doesn't like to talk about it, he says, "But I will say that we have a devised a way to make an instrument 'talk' in the orchestral piece. That opens many, many avenues. The instrument is a kind of synthesizer."

He is speaking here, and has been talking for several years, about an extended instrumental work, and among the projects on which he is working currently is indeed an orchestral suite, which brings to mind the relatively recent trend toward calling Wonder a young Duke Ellington. Ella Fitzgerald may have made the comparison first, but it has been echoed by many others. Musically the comparison may be an apt one, and a tribute to Stevie at such a relatively young age. But there is every likelihood that in the more liberal racial atmosphere and given the more advanced technology of this half of the twentieth century, Stevie Wonder could go beyond comparison with late, great musicians and reach the point where he would become the standard by which all other musical giants are measured.

Certainly his voice is better than Ellington's was, and it would be shortsighted not to consider Stevie's voice as a potential musical force in its own right. On *Songs*, his singing was stronger than it had ever been before, almost magical in its range of style and mood, and his command of the techniques of overdubbing only

serves to increase its possibilities. It has been said before: Stevie Wonder plays his voice like a musical instrument. His richly textured vocals have been and no doubt will continue to be not a small factor in the musical success of his recordings.

Lyrically, however, he lacks Ellington's sophistication. The words to many of his songs reveal a surprising lack of understanding of the politics of the black American experience, not to mention the American experience in general. As it has been remarked many times, he sounds like a 1960s flower child, or a Southern Baptist preacher. His preachifying onstage can be, as one critic put it, as boring as church. At least he is not a hypocrite about it. He talks the same way in private. He has been known to employ the pontifical "we" when a simple "I" would do nicely, and his speech, a combination of music world lingo and California catch-phrasing about communication and togetherness, can cause one to wonder when he is going to "get it together and do

Backstage after the Billboard Number 1 Music Awards in December 1977, Stevie, who got two awards—Male Pop Artist and Top Soul Artist—got together with two fellow winners, Top Jazz Artist George Benson and Top Disco Artist Donna Summer. *(United Press International)*

Lou Rawls, Ella Fitzgerald, Stevie and Cab Calloway were all at the sixteenth annual American Music Awards in January 1978. Stevie won honors as Favorite Male Vocalist and for Favorite Album. Ella, who has called Stevie a young Duke Ellington, received a Distinguished Merit Award at the ceremonies.
(United Press International)

some communicating." Some critics, after pronouncing his thinking in this area simplistic, have suggested that his blindness is a factor. The concepts of love and peace among men have been advanced to all of us, but because most of us can see the gap between ideal and actual, we have chosen not to believe in them. Stevie, on the other hand, has no choice but to believe. "That was the definitive condition of his life," wrote Robert Christgau in 1974. "Much more than you or me, he was in contact with the unconscious acts of faith that get every one of us through each day."

Stevie Wonder does not like to be singled out because of his blindness. "To me, this is normal," he says, and indeed, he is probably the *seeingest* blind man who ever lived. He can be sitting in a room full of people—and frequently is, for he thrives on maximum aural stimulation—and isolate a single conversation amidst the din. Riding in his car through a busy street, he will ask

his driver to stop so he can listen to a record being played down the block, music no one else in the car has been able to hear. In an unfamiliar place, he will be guided by a friend or aide—and end up preventing the other from stumbling. He "watches" television for hours on end, goes to movies often. Backstage at his Madison Square Garden concert in 1974, Andy Warhol brought him a movie camera, and he proceeded to shoot movies of everyone around, identifying their whereabouts by the sounds of their voices. He roller-skates, bowls, and can beat most challengers at Air Hockey. In January 1977 New York police confiscated his two Flash Gordon-type zap guns, which are illegal in New York and New Jersey. The so-called laser weapons look like flashlights but fire darts at the end of copper wires which give the victim a high voltage jolt. With the weapons safely in hand, the officers wanted to know how Stevie could aim the lasers. Easy. As his L.A.

Joseph Eger, left, President of the Symphony for the United Nations (SUN), presented the SUN Peace Award to Stevie in December 1977, as Livingston L. Biddle, Chairman of the National Endowment for the Arts, looked on. Although Stevie has won hundreds of awards, he was especially pleased to receive recognition for his efforts on behalf of the cause of world peace through personal and professional activities. *(Wide World Photos)*

engineer, John Fischbach is fond of saying, "Stevie can hit you with a roll of tape from across the room."

Nevertheless, he lacks that crucial sense, and that lack makes him feel vunerable. He is an intensely private person, elusive, overcautious about things he need not be cautious about. Although he is habitually late, he is chronically late in keeping interview appointments and has been known to keep journalists waiting for weeks. He flatly states that he does not feel he should be of public interest and that if people want to know him all they need do is listen to his music. "It's my music," he says, "my music alone."

Few other musicians have exposed themselves in their work as much as Stevie Wonder has. It is to his credit that he has made such an effort, tries so hard to express in his music what he is as a person, and he has succeeded to a marked degree. One comes away from listening to *Songs in the Key of Life*, for example, really liking the man as well as the music. But the resulting image, though multi-faceted, is still incomplete, and because he has chosen to communicate with the larger world primarily through his music, his awareness of that world is also necessarily incomplete.

For most of his life, Stevie Wonder has been protected, first by Motown, later by well-meaning aides, publicists, lawyers, co-workers, friends. Consequently, his awareness of larger things, things not directly under his control, appears to have come late. This is by no means a call for increased militancy on his part. There are subtle ways in which truths can be told, hypocrisies exposed, greater humanity encouraged. There is a cut on *Songs in the Key of Life* called "*Ngiculela*—Es Una Historia—I Am Singing," that as the title suggests includes verses in Zulu, Spanish and English. Its unspoken exhortation to togetherness is far stronger than an outright call for it. Like no one else on the pop music scene today, Stevie Wonder has the ear of America. He could utilize that power better, either in his music or in his role as a public figure. He has said that respect comes from understanding, and there is much he could do to increase understanding among the races in America by giving voice to the condition of being black in America.

At the New Orleans Jazz & Heritage Festival in April 1977, Stevie joined Ella Fitzgerald onstage for their first performance together. The two sang a duet of Stevie's "You Are the Sunshine of My Life." *(Wide World Photos)*

Perhaps it is wrong to expect such socio-political contributions from those whose popularity is based on contributions in other areas. Even now, Stevie Wonder has done his share of helping and giving, through his charity work and through a hundred acts that do not get publicity or are insufficiently publicized. In July 1977 his former musical director, Lee Garrett, depressed because of money problems, telephoned a Los Angeles mental health center and said he was going to commit suicide, whereupon he locked himself in the bathroom with a revolver. Stevie, who more than most of us knows how precious life is, was notified, went to the apartment, and helped talk Garrett into giving up the gun.

After attending a performance of the Broadway musical "Timbuktu," Stevie went backstage to visit with Eartha Kitt, one of the stars of the show. *(Wide World Photos)*

Thumb through the booklet that accompanies *Songs in the Key of Life*, a booklet that alone must have taken months to produce. Fully ten pages are devoted to credits. For the individual cuts, credit is given not just to the instrumentalists and major background vocalists (including Stevie's younger sister, Renee, who does background on "I Wish"), but to *all* the background people; every single background handclapper in "Isn't She Lovely" is identified by name, as are all the vocalists on such cuts as "Pastime Paradise" and "Black Man." Even the historical figures identified in "Black Man"—from Crispus Attucks through Jan Metzlinger—are listed. For what might be termed "general support" he thanks, among others, Yolanda, Syreeta, his mother and father, his sister and brothers, Yolanda's parents, the Michigan School for the Blind, the Detroit schools he attended, "all the present and former staff of Motown Record Corporation," the doctor who delivered Aisha, "all my aunts, uncles and cousins . . ." He asks everyone's help in the fight to get fair trials for politically powerless people accused of crimes; he speaks of his "mission to spread love mentalism;" he thanks, in alphabetical order, some two hundred individuals, including Kareem Abdul-Jabbar, Sergio Mendes, Melvin Van Peebles and Aisha, for "your time and kindness." It's mind-boggling. The cat is too much. But he's real. Who could make up a man who takes the time to thank nearly everyone he's ever known . . . by name?

Christgau may be right. Because Stevie Wonder cannot see, he must rely on the nonvisual signals he picks up. Those of us who are sighted tend to rely heavily on visual signals. In terms of any prospects for universal love and brotherhood, most of us do not see much hope. Stevie does. Perhaps that does not make him unsophisticated. Perhaps what he senses gives him more cause for hope than what most of us see. Perhaps, though blind physically, spiritually he is the eyes and the ears, the mind and the heart, that we need in our times.

(Kwame Brathwaite)

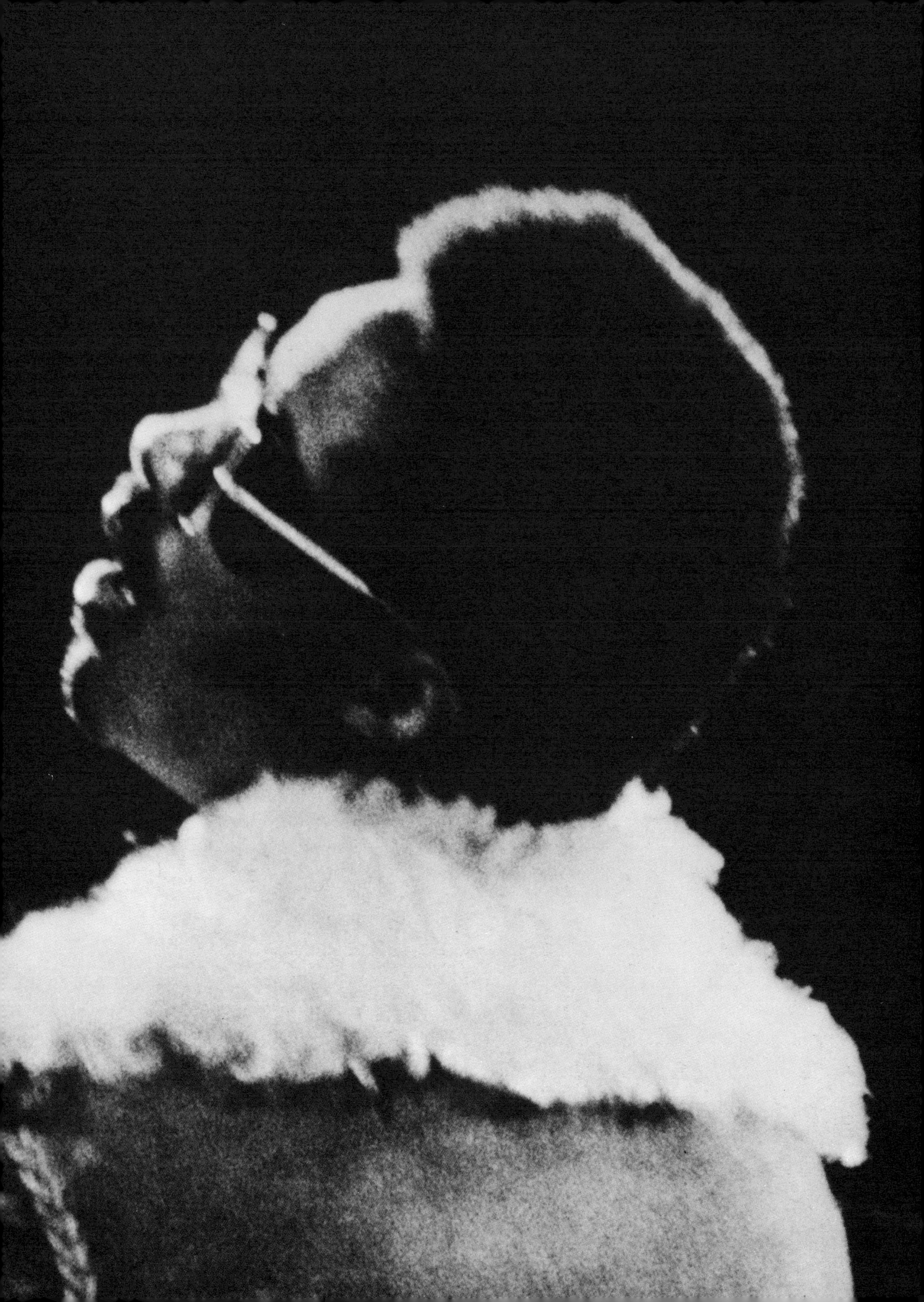

Photo credits (left to right): Globe Photos; Paul Slade, Pictorial Parade; United Press International; Kwame Brathwaite.

BOOKS

Gillett, Charlie. *The Sound of the City: The Rise of Rock and Roll.* New York: E.P. Dutton & Co., 1970.
Haskins, James. *The Story of Stevie Wonder.* New York: Lothrop, Lee & Shepard Co., 1976.
Larkin, Rochelle, *Soul Music!* New York: Lancer Books, Inc., 1970.

ARTICLES

Brown, Geoff. "Innervisions." *Melody Maker.* February 2, 1974, pp. 36-37.
Brown, Geoff. "Stevie Wonder: The New Sound of Soul," *Melody Maker.* June 22, 1974, pp. 31-37.
Christgau, Robert. "Stevie Wonder is a Fool." *Village Voice.* December 16, 1974.
Christgau, Robert. "Stevie Wonder is a Masterpiece." *Village Voice.* November 8, 1976, p. 50.
Clark, Sue C. "Stevie Wonder Gets Good and Pissed." *Rolling Stone.* September 30, 1971, p. 12.
Dove, Ian. "Stevie Wonder's 'Most Personal' D." New York *Times.* July 19, 1973.
Driscoll, O'Connell. "Growing Up Stevie Wonder." *Rolling Stone.* June 19, 1975, pp. 44-47+.
Eldridge, Royston. "Funkedelic!" *Melody Maker.* March 15, 1969. p. 7.
Eldridge, Royston. "Stevie Gets His No. 1." *Melody Maker.* December 20, 1969, p. 7.
Eldridge, Royston. "Will Stevie Wonder Become Another Sammy Davis."*Melody Maker.* February 15, 1969, p. 7.
Heckman, Don. "Stevie Wonder to Open Stones Concert at Garden." New York *Times.* July 24, 1972, p. 17.
Holden, Stephen. "Stevie Wonder Says It All." *Billboard.* February, 1977, pp. 141-142.
"It's Not Such a Drag Being Blind." *Melody Maker.* October 14, 1967, p. 11.
Landau, John. "Motown." *Rolling Stone.* December 14, 1967, p. 19.
Mancini, Anthony. "The Wonderful World of Stevie." New York *Post.* July 22, 1975, p. 15.
Moore, Carman. "Wonder: Warmed-Up to a Crisp." *Village Voice.* August 3, 1972.
Plummer, Mark. "Stevie Freaks Out." *Melody Maker.* January 30, 1971, p. 7.
Plummer, Mark. "The Boy Wonder." *Melody Maker,* July 18, 1970.

  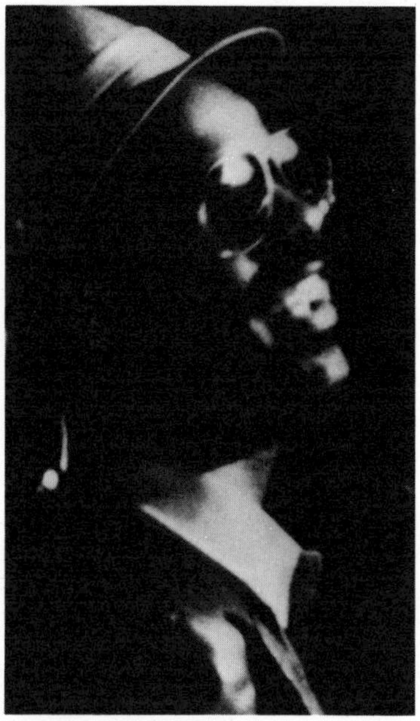 

Photo credits (left to right); United Press International; Wide World Photos; Wide World Photos; United Press International.

Robins, Wayne. "Further Fulfillingness." *Melody Maker.* November 9, 1974, p. 59.
Rockwell, John. "For Stevie Wonder, A New Life Dawns." New York *Times.* March 22, 1974, p. 34.
Rockwell, John. "Pop Music Found to Renew Itself." New York *Times.* March 16, 1975.
Rockwell, John. "Stevie Wonder Wins 4 Grammys." New York *Times.* February 21, 1977, p. 42.
Rockwell, John. "The Exhilarating Freshness of Stevie Wonder." New York *Times.* October 17, 1976, pp. 17-18.
Rockwell, John. "Wonder is at Center of Black Music." New York *Times.* March 27, 1974.
Slater, Jack. "A Sense of Wonder." New York *Times* Magazine. February 23, 1975, pp. 18.
Slater, Jack. "Stevie Wonder: The Genius of the Man and His Music."*Ebony.* January, 77, pp. 29-32.
Snider, Burr. "Hey, Stevie Wonder, How's Your Bad Self?" *Esquire.* April, 1974, pp. 100-102.
"Steve Talk" *Melody Maker.* September 2, 1967, p. 5
Swenson, John. "In Synch with the Shaman." *Village Voice.* April 11, 1974.
Underwood, Lee. "Boy Wonder Grows Up." *Down Beat.* September 12, 1974, pp. 14-15.
Ward, Ed. "Jamaican 'Dream' Show: Will Wonder Never Cease?" *Rolling Stone.* June 19, 1975, pp. 44-47.
Wickham, Vicki. "Wonder Bounces Back." *Melody Maker.* September 22, 1973, p. 3.
Willis, Ellen. "The Importance of Stevie Wonder." *The New Yorker.* December 30, 1974.
Wilson, John S. "Big Stevie Wonder Serves Soul at Philharmonic Hall." New York *Times,* September 27, 1969.
"Wonderful World of Stevie Wonder," *Ebony,* vol. 18 #9. July, 1963, p. 14.

EPHEMERA

Melody Maker	1966-1977
Rolling Stone	1966-1977
The New York Times	1966-1977
The Village Voice	1966-1977
Variety	1966-1977

Photograph on following page © 1978 by Kwame Brathwaite.